USE
YOUR
PERFECT
MEMORY

Tony Buzan

E.P. DUTTON, Inc.   New York

Published in the United States by E.P. Dutton, Inc.,
2 Park Avenue, New York, N.Y. 10016

Library of Congress Cataloging in Publication Data
Buzan, Tony.
 Use your perfect memory.
 1. Mnemonics. I. Title.
BF371.B88 1984   153.1'4   83-20771

153
B

ISBN: 0-525-48112-5

10 9 8 7 6 5 4 3 2 1

To Zeus and Mnemosyne's Ideal Muse-Child:
my dear, dear friend Lorraine Gill, the Artist

Contents

Introduction

Like so many children, as a youth I was mystified by this wonderful and exasperating thing called memory. In casual and relaxed situations it worked so smoothly that we hardly ever noticed it; in examinations it only occasionally performed well, to our surprise, but was more often associated with "bad memory," the fearful area of forgetting. Since I spent much of my childhood in the country with animals, I began to realize that the misnamed "dumb" creatures seemed to have extraordinary memories, often superior to our own. Why, then, was human memory apparently so faulty?

I began to study in earnest, eagerly devouring information about how the early Greeks had devised specific memory systems for various tasks; and how, later, the Romans applied these techniques to enable themselves to remember whole books of mythology and to impress their audiences during senatorial speeches and debates. My interest became more focused while I was in college, when the realization slowly dawned on me that such basic systems need not be used only for "rote" or parrotlike memory, but could be used as gigantic filing systems for the mind, enabling extraordinarily fast and efficient access, and enormously enhancing general understanding. I applied the techniques in taking examinations, to winning bets on how many things I could memorize in both forward and reverse order, in playing games with my imagination in order to improve my memory, and in helping other students who were supposedly on the road to academic failure achieve first-class successes.

The explosion of brain research during the last decade has confirmed what the memory theorists, gamesters, mnemonic technicians, and magicians have always known: that the holding capacity of our brains and the ability to recall what is held and stored there are far and deliciously beyond our normal expectations.

Use Your Perfect Memory is an initial tour through what should have been included as first among the seven wonders of the world: the "hanging gardens" of limitless memory and imagination.

USE
YOUR
PERFECT
MEMORY

1

Is Your Memory Perfect?

Your memory is phenomenal.

This statement is made despite the following counterarguments:

1. Most people remember fewer than 10 percent of the names of those whom they meet.

2. Most people forget more than 99 percent of the phone numbers given to them.

3. Memory is supposed to decline rapidly with age.

4. Many people drink, and alcohol is reputed to destroy one thousand brain cells per drink.

5. Internationally, across races, cultures, ages, and education levels, there is a common experience, and fear of, having an inadequate or bad memory.

6. Our failures in general and especially in remembering are attributed to the fact that we are "only human," a statement that implies that our skills are inherently inadequate.

7. You will probably fail most of the memory tests in the following chapter.

Points 1, 2, and 7 will be dealt with through the remainder of the book. You will see that it is possible, with appropriate knowledge, to pass all the tests, and that names and phone numbers are easy to remember—if you know how.

Your memory does decline with age, but only if it is not used. Conversely, if it is used, it will continue to improve throughout your lifetime.

There is no evidence to suggest that moderate drinking destroys brain cells. This misapprehension arose because it was found that excessive drinking, and only excessive drinking, did indeed damage the brain.

Across cultural and international boundaries "negative experience" with memory can be traced not to our being "only human" or in any way innately inadequate but to two simple, easily changeable factors: (1) negative mental set and (2) lack of knowledge.

Negative Mental Set

There is a growing and informal international organization, which I choose to name the "I've Got an Increasingly Bad Memory Club." How often do you hear people in animated and enthusiastic conversation saying things like "You know, my memory's not nearly as good as it used to be when I was younger; I'm constantly forgetting things." To which there is an equally enthusiastic reply: "Yes, I know exactly what you mean; the same thing's happening to me. . . ." And off they dodder, arms draped around each other's shoulders, down the hill to mental oblivion. And such conversations often take place between thirty-year-olds!

This negative, dangerous, *incorrect* mental set is based on lack of proper training, and this book is designed to correct it.

Consider the younger supermemorizer to whom most people romantically refer. If you want to check for yourself, go back to any school at the end of a day, walk into a classroom of a group of five- to seven-year-old children after they have gone home and ask the teacher what has been left in the classroom (i.e., forgotten). You will find the following items: watches, pencils, pens, sweets and candy, money, jackets, physical education equipment, books, coats, wallets, glasses, erasers, toys, etc.

The only real difference between the middle-aged executive who has forgotten to phone someone he was supposed to phone and who has left his briefcase at the office, and the seven-year-old child who returns home having realized that he's left at school his watch, his pocketmoney, and his homework is that the seven-year-old does not collapse into depression, clutching his head and exclaiming, "Oh, Christ, I'm seven years old and my memory's going!"

Ask yourself "What is the number of things I actually remember each day?" Most people estimate somewhere between one hundred and ten thousand. The answer is in fact in the multiple billions. The human memory is so excellent and runs so smoothly that most people don't even realize that every word they speak and every word they listen to are instantaneously produced for consideration, recalled, recognized precisely, and placed in their appropriate context. Nor do they realize that every moment, every perception, every thought, *everything* that they do throughout the entire day and throughout their lives is a function of their memories. In fact, its ongoing accuracy is almost perfect. The few odd things that we do forget are like odd specks on a gigantic ocean. Ironically, the reason why we notice so dramatically the errors that we make is because they are so rare.

There is now inceasing evidence that our memories may not only be far better than we ever thought but may in fact be perfect. Consider the following arguments for this case:

1. Dreams

Many people have vivid dreams of acquaintances, friends, family, and lovers of whom they have not thought for as many as twenty to forty years. In their dreams, however, the images are *perfectly* clear, all colors and details being exactly as they were in real life. This confirms that somewhere in the brain there is a vast storage of perfect images and associations that does not change with time and that, with the right trigger, can be recalled. In chapter 26 you will learn about Catching Your Dreams.

2. Surprise Random Recall

Practically everyone has had the experience of turning a corner and suddenly recalling people or events from previous times in his life. This often happens when people revisit their first school. A single smell, touch, sight, or sound can bring back a flood of experiences thought to be forgotten. This ability of any given sense to reproduce perfect memory images indicates that if there were more correct "trigger situations," much more would and could be recollected. We know from such experiences that the brain has retained the information.

3. The Russian "S"

In the early part of this century a young Russian journalist (in *The Mind of a Mnemonist* by A. R. Luria, he is referred to as "S") attended an editorial meeting, and it was noted to the consternation of others that he was not taking notes. When pressed to explain, he became confused; to everyone's amazement, it became apparent that he really did not understand why anyone should ever take notes. The explanation that he gave for not taking notes himself was that he could remember what the editor was saying, so what was the point? Upon being challenged, "S" reproduced the entire speech, word for word, sentence for sentence, and inflection for inflection.

For the next thirty years he was to be tested and examined by Alexander Luria, Russia's leading psychologist and expert on memory. Luria confirmed that "S" was in no way abnormal but that his memory was indeed perfect. Luria also stated that at a very young age "S" had "stumbled upon" the basic mnemonic principles (see pages 40ff.) and that they had become part of his natural functioning.

"S" was not unique. The history of education, medicine, and psychology is dotted with similar cases of perfect memorizers. In every instance, their brains were found to be normal, and in every instance they had, as young children, "discovered" the basic principles of their memory's function.

4. Professor Rosensweig's Experiments

Professor Mark Rosensweig, a Californian psychologist and neurophysiologist, spent years studying the individual brain cell and its capacity for storage. As early as 1974 he stated that if we fed in ten new items of information *every second* for an entire lifetime to any normal human brain that brain would be considerably less than half full. He emphasized that memory problems have nothing to do with the capacity of the brain but rather with the self-management of that apparently limitless capacity.

5. Professor Penfield's Experiments

Professor Wilde Penfield of Canada came across his discovery of the capacity of human memory by mistake. Professor Penfield was stimulating individual brain cells wih tiny electrodes for the purpose of locating areas of the brain that were the cause of patients' epilepsy.

To his amazement he found that when he stimulated certain individual brain cells, his patients were suddenly recalling experiences from their past. The patients emphasized that it was not simple memory, but that they actually were reliving the entire experience, including smells, noises, colors, movement, tastes. These experiences ranged from a few hours before the experimental session to as much as 40 years earlier.

Penfield suggested that hidden within each brain cell or cluster of brain cells lies a perfect storage of every event of our past and that if we could find the right stimulus we could replay the entire film.

6. The Potential Pattern-Making Ability of Your Brain

Professor Pyotr Anokhin, the famous Pavlov's brightest student, spent his last years investigating the potential pattern-making capabilities of the human brain. His findings were important for memory researchers. It seems that memory is recorded in separate little patterns, or electromagnetic circuits, that are formed by the brain's interconnecting cells.

Anokhin already knew that the brain contained a million million brain cells (1,000,000,000,000) but that even this gigantic number was going to be small in comparison to the number of patterns that those brain cells could make among themselves. Working with advanced electron microscopes and computers, he came up with a staggering number. Anokhin calculated that the number of patterns, or "degrees of freedom" throughout the brain, is, to use his own words, "so great that writing it would take a line of figures, in normal manuscript characters, more than ten and a half million *kilometers* in length. With such a number of possibilities, the brain is a keyboard on which hundreds of millions of different melodies can be played."

Your memory is the music.

7. Death-Type Experiences

Many people have looked up at the surface ripples of a swimming pool from the bottom, knowing that they were going to drown within the next two minutes; or seen the rapidly disappearing ledge of the mountain from which they have just fallen; or felt the oncoming grid of the ten-ton truck bearing down on them at 60 miles per hour. A common theme runs through the accounts that survivors of such traumas tell. In such moments of "final consideration" the brain slows all things down to a standstill, expanding a fraction of a second into a lifetime, and reviews the *total* experience of the individual.

When pressed to admit that what they had really experienced were a few highlights, the individuals concerned insisted that what they had experienced was their *entire* life, including all things they had completely forgotten until that instant of time. "My whole life flashed before me" has almost become a cliché that goes with the near-death experience. Such a commonality of experience again argues for a storage capacity of the brain that we have only just begun to tap.

8. Photographic Memory

Photographic, or eidetic, memory is a specific phenomenon in which people can remember, usually for a very short time, perfectly and exactly anything they have seen. This memory usually fades, but it can be so accurate as to enable somebody, after seeing a picture of a thousand randomly sprayed dots on a white sheet, to reproduce them perfectly. This suggests that in addition to the deep, long-term storage capacity, we also have a shorter term and immediate photographic ability. It is argued that children often have this ability as a natural part of their mental functioning and that we train it away by forcing them to concentrate too much on logic and language and too little on imagination and their other range of mental skills.

9. The Ten Thousand Photographs

In recent experiments people were shown a thousand photographs, one after the other, at a pace of about one photograph per second. The psychologists then mixed one hundred photographs with the original one thousand, and asked the people to select those they had not seen the first time through. Everyone, regardless of how he described his normal memory, was able to identify almost every photograph he had seen—as well as each one that he had not seen previously. They were not necessarily able to remember the order in which the photographs had been presented, but they could definitely remember the image—an example that confirms the common human experience of being better able to remember a face than the name attached to it. This particular problem is easily dealt with by applying the Memory Techniques.

10. The Memory Techniques

The memory techniques, or mnemonics (see\page 41), were a system of "memory codes" that enabled people to remember perfectly whatever it was they wished to remember. Experiments with these techniques have shown that if a person scores 9 out of 10 when using such a technique, that same person will score 900 out of 1,000, 9,000 out of 10,000 and 900,000 out of 1,000,000 and so on. Similarly, one who scores perfectly out of ten will score perfectly out of 1,000,000. These techniques help us to delve into that phenomenal storage capacity we have and to pull out whatever it is that we need. The basic memory principles are outlined in chapter 4, and the bulk of this book is devoted to explaining and outlining the most important and useful of these systems, showing how easily they can be learned, and how they can be applied in personal, family, business, and community life.

At this early stage, however, it should be helpful for you to test your memory in its current state. The following chapter provides a series of memory tests that will form a foundation from which you can check your progress. If you are interested in the truth about yourself and your performance now, as compared with what it will be when you have completed the book, perform these tests thoroughly. Most people do rather poorly at the beginning and almost perfectly at the end.

2

Testing Your Current Memory Capabilities

Few people ever put their memories to the immediate test, and it is for this reason that most are unaware of the false limits, the habits, and potential of their minds. Because of the way we are trained (or not trained) in school, the simple tasks you will soon attempt will in some cases prove very difficult and in others almost impossible. Yet these tasks are perfectly within the capacity of the average human brain. Do not worry about poor performance, however, since it is the purpose of this book to make memorization, such as is required in the following tests, an easy and enjoyable exercise.

Link Test

Read the following list of twenty objects through *once* only, trying to memorize both the objects and the order in which they are listed.

Wallpaper
Mountain
Skirt
String
Ice cream
Scissors
Nail
Watch
Nurse
Perfume
Elephant
Jail
Mirror
Suitcase
Plant
Power
Safe
Melon
Mongrel
Engraving

Now turn to page 19 to test yourself and for scoring instructions.

Peg Test

Give yourself sixty seconds to remember this second list of twenty items. The aim in this test is to remember the items in random order, connecting them to their apropriate number. When your minute has passed, turn to pages 20 and 21.

1. Atom
2. Tree
3. Stethoscope
4. Sofa
5. Alley
6. Tile
7. Windscreen
8. Honey
9. Brush
10. Toothpaste
11. Glitter
12. Heater
13. Railway
14. Lighter
15. Wart
16. Star
17. Peace
18. Button
19. Pram
20. Pump

Face Test

Look at the ten faces on the following two pages for not more than two minutes, then turn to pages 22 and 23 where the same faces are presented without their names. Try to match the right name to the right face. Turn to page 23 for scoring.

Mrs. Whitehead

Mr. Hawkins

Mr. Knight

Mr. Ramm

Mrs. Hemming

Mrs. Briar

Mr. Chester

Mr. Masters

Mrs. Swanson

Miss Temple

Number Test

Look at the four 15-digit numbers printed below, giving not more than a half-minute to each. At the end of each half-minute section turn to page 24 and write down the number as best you can.

1. 798465328185423
2. 493875941254945
3. 784319884385628
4. 825496581198762

Telephone Number Test

The following is a list of ten people and their telephone numbers. Study the list for not more than two minutes and attempt to remember all the phone numbers, then turn to page 25 and answer the appropriate questions.

Your local butcher	487-3245
Your dentist	324-7646
Your bank manager	878-7251
Your doctor	931-6898
Your local grocer	545-2363
Your local pharmacist	886-6129
Your tennis partner	456-7971
Your plumber	529-6253
Your local bar	939-2853
Your garage	914-1363

The Card Test

This test is designed to exercise your present capacity in remembering cards and their sequence. The list below contains all fifty-two cards of the regular pack in numbered order. Your task is to spend not more than three minutes looking at this list, and then to recall it in order.

1. Ten of diamonds
2. Ace of spades
3. Three of hearts
4. Jack of clubs
5. Five of clubs
6. Five of hearts
7. Six of hearts
8. Eight of clubs
9. Ace of clubs
10. Queen of clubs
11. King of spades
12. Ten of hearts
13. Six of clubs
14. Three of diamonds
15. Four of spades
16. Four of clubs
17. Queen of hearts
18. Five of spades
19. Jack of diamonds
20. Seven of hearts
21. Nine of clubs
22. King of diamonds
23. Seven of clubs
24. Two of spades
25. Jack of hearts
26. King of clubs
27. Four of hearts
28. Two of diamonds
29. Jack of spades
30. Six of spades
31. Two of hearts
32. Four of diamonds
33. Three of spades
34. Eight of diamonds
35. Ace of hearts
36. Queen of spades

37. Queen of diamonds
38. Six of diamonds
39. Nine of spades
40. Ten of clubs
41. King of hearts
42. Nine of hearts
43. Eight of spades
44. Seven of spades

45. Three of clubs
46. Ace of diamonds
47. Ten of spades
48. Eight of hearts
49. Seven of diamonds
50. Nine of diamonds
51. Two of clubs
52. Five of diamonds

Now turn to page 26 and fill in the answers.

Dates Test

This is your last test: Listed below are ten fairly important historical dates. Give yourself two minutes to remember them all perfectly.

1. 1666   Fire of London
2. 1770   Beethoven's birthday
3. 1215   Signing of Magna Carta
4. 1917   Russian Revolution
5. c. 1454   First printing press
6. 1815   Battle of Waterloo
7. 1608   Invention of the telescope
8. 1905   Einstein's theory of relativity
9. 1789   French Revolution
10. 1776   American Declaration of Independence

Now turn to page 27.

Link Test Response
(See p. 10)

1. Note in the space provided all the words you remembered, in correct order.

Score yourself in two ways: First enter below the number of items you remembered out of twenty, and then record the number of items you listed in the correct order. (If you reversed two items, they are both wrong with regard to order.) Score one point for each remembered; one point for each correct placing (total possible: 40).

Number remembered:＿＿＿ Number incorrect:＿＿＿＿

Number in correct order:＿＿ Number in incorrect order:＿

Peg Test Response
(See p. 11)

In the order indicated, place the word you were given next to its appropriate number.

20

18

16

14

12

10

8

6

4

2

1

3

5

7

9

11

13

15

17

19

Number correct: _____

Face Test Response
(See pp. 12 and 13)

Fit the Names to the Faces:

8

7

6

1

5

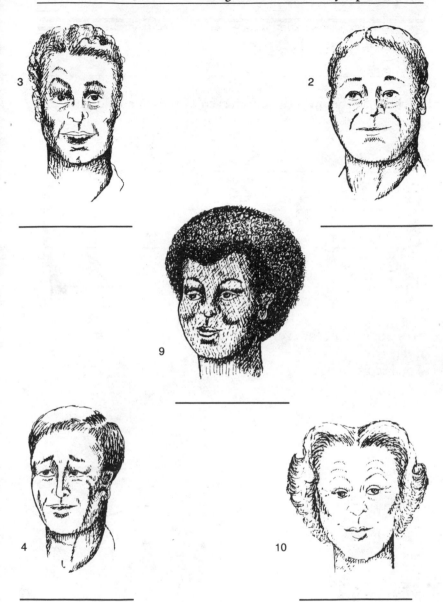

SCORING INSTRUCTIONS: Score one point for each correct answer.

Number Test Response
(See p. 14)

In the space below write down each of the four 15-digit numbers.

1. _____

2. _____

3. _____

4. _____

Score one point for every number that you record *in its proper sequence*.

Total score: ____

60

Telephone Number Test Response
(See p. 15)

Write down, in the space provided, the phone numbers of the ten people.

NAME	NUMBER
1. Your local butcher	
2. Your dentist	
3. Your bank manager	
4. Your doctor	
5. Your local grocer	
6. Your local pharmacist	
7. Your tennis partner	
8. Your plumber	
9. Your local bar	
10. Your garage	

Scoring: Give yourself one mark for each correct number (even if you make one mistake only in the number you must consider this totally wrong, for if you had dialed it you would not have been put in contact with the person with whom you wished to speak. The highest possible score is 10).

Score: ____

10

Card Test Response
(See pp. 16 and 17)

Recall the list in reverse order as indicated.

52.	26.
51.	25.
50.	24.
49.	23.
48.	22.
47.	21.
46.	20.
45.	19.
44.	18.
43.	17.
42.	16.
41.	15.
40.	14.
39.	13.
38.	12.
37.	11.
36.	10.
35.	9.
34.	8.
33.	7.
32.	6.
31.	5.
30.	4.
29.	3.
28.	2.
27.	1.

Score one point for each correct answer. A score of 52 is perfect.

Dates Test Response
(See p. 18)

9. _____ French Revolution
6. _____ Battle of Waterloo
1. _____ Fire of London
10. _____ American Declaration of Independence
2. _____ Beethoven's birthday
5. _____ First printing press
4. _____ Russian Revolution
3. _____ Signing of Magna Carta
8. _____ Einstein's theory of relativity
7. _____ Invention of the telescope

Scoring: Give yourself one point for an accurate answer and half a point if you come within five years. Ten points is a perfect score.

Now calculate your total score—perfect is 202.

This completes your initial testing (there will be other tests for you to experiment with throughout the text). Normal scores on each of these tests range from 20 and 60 percent. Even a score of 60 percent, which in the average group will be considered excellent, is well below what you can expect of yourself when you have absorbed the information in this book. The average trained memorizer would have scores between 95 and 100 percent on every one of the foregoing tests.

The next chapter outlines the history of memory, giving you a context in which to learn the memory techniques and systems, and shows how recently it is that we have begun to understand your amazing innate abilities.

Test Result Summary

TEST	YOUR SCORE	POSSIBLE TOTAL
Link Test		40
Peg Test		20
Face Test		10
Number Test		60
Telephone Number Test		10
Card Test		52
Dates Test		10
		202

Summary Percent Score:

3

The History of Memory

From the time when man first began to depend on his mind for coping with his environment, the possession of an excellent memory has been a step to positions of command and respect. Throughout human history there have been recorded remarkable—sometimes legendary—feats of memory.

The Greeks

It is difficult to say exactly when and where the first integrated ideas on memory arose. The first sophisticated concepts, however, can be attributed to the Greeks, some six hundred years before the birth of Christ. As we look back on them now, these "sophisticated" ideas were surprisingly naïve, especially since some of the men proposing them are numbered among the greatest thinkers the world has ever known.

In the sixth century B.C., Parmenides thought of memory as being a mixture of light and dark or heat and cold. He thought that as long as any given mixture remained unstirred, the memory would be perfect. As soon as the mixture was altered, forgetting occurred. Diogenes of Appollonia advanced a different theory, in the fifth century B.C. He suggested that memory was a process that consisted of events producing an equal distribution of air in the body. Like Parmenides, he thought that when this equilibrium was disturbed, forgetting would occur.

Not surprisingly, the first person to introduce a really major idea in the field of memory was Plato, in the fourth century B.C. His theory is known as the Wax Tablet Hypothesis and is still accepted by some people today, although there is growing disagreement. To Plato, the mind accepted impressions in the same way that wax becomes marked when a pointed object is applied to its surface. Plato assumed that once the impression had been made it remained until it wore away with time, leaving a smooth surface once again. This smooth surface was, of course, what Plato considered to be equivalent to complete forgetting—the opposite aspect of the same process. As will become clear later, many people now feel that memory and forgetting are two quite different processes. Shortly after Plato, Zeno the Stoic slightly modified Plato's ideas, suggesting that sensations actually "wrote" impressions on the wax tablet. Like the Greeks before him, when Zeno referred to the mind and its memory, he did not place it in any particular organ or section of the body. To him as to the Greeks, "mind" was a very unclear concept.

The first man to introduce a more scientific terminology was Aristotle, in the late fourth century B.C. He maintained that the language previously used was not adequate to explain the physical aspects of memory. In applying his new language Aristotle attributed to the heart most of the functions that we now attribute to the brain. Part of the heart's function, he realized, was concerned with the blood, and he felt that memory was based on the blood's movements. He thought that forgetting was the result of a gradual slowing down of these movements. Aristotle made another important contribution to the subject of memory when he introduced his laws of association of ideas. The concept of association of ideas and images is now known to be of major importance to memory. Throughout this book this concept will be discussed and applied.

In the third century B.C., Herophilus introduced "vital" and "animal" spirits to the discussion. He thought that the vital, or "higher order," spirits produced the "lower order" animal spirits, which included the memory, the brain, and the nervous system. All of these he thought to be secondary in importance to the heart. It is interesting to note that one reason advanced by Herophilus for man's superiority over animals was the large number of creases in his brain. (These creases are now known as the convolutions of the cortex.) Herophilus, however, offered no reason for his conclusion. It was not until the nineteenth century, more than two thousand years later, that the real importance of the cortex was discovered.

The Greeks, then, were the first to seek a physical as opposed to a spiritual basis for memory; they developed scientific concepts and a language structure that helped the development of these concepts; and they contributed the Wax Tablet Hypothesis, which suggested that memory and forgetting were opposite aspects of the same process.

The Romans

The theoretical contributions by the Romans to our knowledge of memory were surprisingly minimal. The major thinkers of their time, including Cicero in the first century B.C. and Quintilian in the first century A.D., accepted without question the Wax Tablet Hypothesis of memory and did little further work on the subject. Their major and extremely important contributions were in the development of memory systems. They were the first to introduce the idea of a Link System and a Room System, both of which will be described in later chapters.

The Influence of the Christian Church

The next major contributor to memory theory was the great physician Galen in the second century A.D. He located and delineated various anatomical and physiological structures and made further investigations into the function and structure of the nervous system. Like the later Greeks, he assumed that memory and mental processes were part of the lower order of animal spirits. He thought that these spirits were manufactured in the sides of the brain and that, consequently, memory was seated there. Galen thought that air was sucked into the brain and mixed with the vital spirits. This mixture produced animal spirits that were pushed down through the nervous system, enabling humans to experience sensation.

Galen's ideas on memory were rapidly accepted and condoned by the church, which at this time was beginning to exert a great influence. His ideas became doctrine, and as a result little progress was made in the field for fifteen hundred years. These intellectual strictures stifled some of the greatest minds that philosophy and science have produced. In the fourth century A.D. St. Augustine accepted the church's idea that memory was a function of the soul and that the soul was located in the brain. He never expanded on the anatomical aspects of these ideas.

From the time of St. Augustine until the seventeenth century there were almost no significant developments, and even in the seventeenth century new ideas were restricted by doctrine. Even so great a thinker as Descartes accepted Galen's basic ideas, although he thought that animal spirits were sent from the pineal gland on special courses through the brain until they came to the part where memory could be triggered. The more clear-cut these courses, the more readily, he thought, would they open when animal spirits traveled through them. It was in this way that he explained the improvement of memory and the development of what are known as memory traces. A memory trace is a physical change in the nervous system that was not present before learning. The trace enables us to recall.

Another great philosopher, who went along with the tide, was Thomas Hobbes, who discussed and considered the idea of memory but contributed little to what had already been said. He agreed with Aristotle's ideas, rejecting nonphysical explanations of memory. He did not, however, specify the real nature of memory, nor did he make any significant attempts to locate it accurately.

It is evident from the theories of the sixteenth-century intellectuals that the inhibiting influence of Galen and the church had been profound. Practically all these great thinkers accepted without question primitive ideas on memory.

Transitional Period—the Eighteenth Century

One of the first thinkers to be influenced by the Renaissance and by the ideas of Newton was David Hartley, who developed the vibratory theory of memory. Applying Newton's ideas on vibrating particles, Hartley suggested that there were memory vibrations in the brain that began before birth. New sensations modified existing vibrations in degree, kind, place, and direction. After being influenced by a new sensation, vibrations quickly returned to their natural state. But if the same sensation appeared again, the vibrations took a little longer to return. This progression would finally result in the vibrations remaining in their "new" state, and a memory trace was thus established.

Other major thinkers of this period included Zanotti, who was the first to link electrical forces with brain functions, and Bonnet, who developed the ideas of Hartley in relation to the flexibility of nerve fibers. He felt that the more often nerves were used, the more easily they vibrated, and the better memory would be. The theories of these men were more sophisticated than previous ones because they had been largely influenced by developments in related scientific fields. This interaction of ideas laid the groundwork for some of the modern theories of memory.

The Nineteenth Century

With the development of science in Germany in the nineteenth century, some important advances occurred. Many of the ideas initiated by the Greeks were overthrown, and work on memory expanded to include the biological sciences.

Georg Prochaska, a Czech physiologist, finally and irrevocably rejected the age-old idea of animal spirits on the grounds that it has no scientific basis and that there is no evidence to support it. He felt that limited existing knowledge made speculation on the location of memory in the brain a waste of time. "Spatial localization may be possible," he said, "but we just do not know enough at the moment to make it a useful idea." It was not for some fifty years that localizing the area of memory function became a useful pursuit.

Another major theory presented in this century was that of Pierre Flourens, a French physiologist, who "located" the memory in every part of the brain. He said that the brain acted as a whole and could not be considered as the interaction of elementary parts.

Modern Theories

Modern developments in memory have been aided to an enormous degree by advances in technology and methodology. Almost without exception psychologists and other thinkers in this field agree that memory is located in the cerebrum, which is the large area of the brain covering the surface of the cortex. Even today, however, the exact localization of memory areas is proving a difficult task, as is the accurate understanding of the function of memory itself. Current thought has progressed from Hermann Ebbinghaus's work, at the turn of the century, with regard to basic learning and forgetting curves (see chapter 25) to advanced and complex theories. Research and theory can be roughly divided into three main areas: work on establishing a biochemical basis for memory; theories suggesting that memory can no longer be considered as a single process but must be broken down into divisions; and the clinical surgeon Wilder Penfield's work on brain stimulation.

Research into the biochemical basis for memory was initiated in the late 1950s. This theory suggests that RNA (ribonucleic acid), a complex molecule, serves as a chemical mediator for memory. RNA is produced by the substance DNA (deoxyribonucleic acid), which is responsible for our genetic inheritance. For example, DNA determines eye color. A number of experiments have been performed with RNA that lend support to the idea that RNA does indeed have a lot to do with the way in which we remember things. In one instance, when animals were given certain types of training, the RNA found in specific cells was changed. And further, if the production of RNA in an animal's body was stopped or modified, this animal was unable to learn or remember. An even more exciting experiment showed that when RNA was taken from one rat and injected into another, the second rat "remembered" things that he had never been taught but that the first rat had.

While research into this aspect of memory is progressing, other theorists are saying that we should stop emphasizing "memory" and concentrate more on the study of "forgetting." It is their position that we do not so much remember as gradually forget. Encompassing this idea is the duplex theory of remembering and forgetting, which states that there are two different kinds of information retention: long-term and short-term. For example, you have probably experienced a different "feeling" in the way that you recall a telephone number that has just been given to you and the way that you recall your own telephone number. The short-term situation is one in which the idea is "in" the brain but has not yet been properly coded and is therefore more readily forgotten. In the long-term situation the idea has been completely coded, filed, and stored, and it will probably remain there for years, if not for life.

Research into direct brain stimulation was initiated by Dr. Wilder Penfield. In more detail: when performing craniotomies (removal of a small section of the brain) in order to reduce epileptic attacks, Penfield had first to remove a portion of the skull lying over the side of the brain. Before operating, Penfield conducted a systematic electrical stimulation of the open brain, and the patient, who remained conscious, reported his experience after each stimulation. In an early case Penfield stimulated the temporal lobe of the brain, and the patient reported a re-created memory of a childhood experience.

Penfield found that stimulating various areas of the cortex produces a range of responses but that only stimulation of the temporal lobes leads to reports of meaningful and integrated experiences. These experiences are often complete in that when re-created they include the color, sound, movement, and emotional content of the original experiences.

Of particular interest in these studies is the fact that some of the memories stimulated electrically by Penfield had been unavailable in normal recall. In addition, the stimulated experiences seemed to be far more specific and accurate than normal conscious recall, which tends to be a generalization. It was Penfield's belief that the brain records every item to which it pays conscious attention and that this record is basically permanent, although it may be "forgotten" in day-to-day living.

More recently, theorists have returned to a position similar to that of Flourens, in which they are suggesting that every part of the brain may include *all* memories. This model is based on holographic photography. In simple terms, a holographic photographic plate is simply a piece of glass, which, when two laser beams are passed through it at the right angle, reproduce a ghostly, three-dimensional photograph. One of the amazing things about this photographic plate is that if you smash it into a hundred pieces and take any one of those hundred pieces, you can shine the two laser beams through it and still get the same (although slightly more blurred) picture.

Thus every part of the holographic photographic plate contains a minirecord of the overall picture.

British scientist David Bohm and others are suggesting that the brain is similar. In other words, every one of our multimillion brain cells may, in fact, act as a minibrain, recording in some fantastically complex way as yet indiscernible to our clumsy measuring instruments the entire of our experience. Fantastic as this theory may sound, it goes a long way toward explaining the perfect memories we have in dreams, the surprise random recall, the memories of the perfect memorizers, the statistics from Rosensweig's experiment, the results of Penfield's experiments, the mathematical grandeur of Anokhin's results, and much of the near-death-type experiences.

Even now we are still on the threshold of a wondrous new world of knowledge, similar to that of the first people who began to explore our planet immediately after having discovered that they could make boats.

How Many Brains?

Supplementing this modern research has been the new discovery that we have not one brain but two. Professor Roger Sperry recently received the Nobel Prize for his breakthrough work in this area. Sperry discovered that each one of us has a brain that is divided into two physiological sections, each dealing with a different mental function.

In most of us, the left side of the brain deals with the following areas:

logic
language
number
sequencing and lineality
analysis

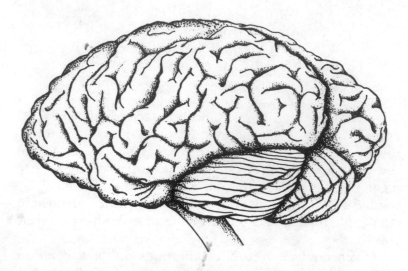

This is your superstreamlined brain, depicted as if viewed with X-ray eyes from a vantage point to the left of the left shoulder. Thus, you are looking at the left hemisphere, which deals with the mental functions of logic, language, number, sequencing and linearity, and analysis. The right side of the brain, the back tip of which you can just see, deals with rhythm and music, imagination, daydreaming, color, and dimension. The combination of these two ranges of abilities combine to give you a superpowered memory.

Similarly, in most of us, the right side of the brain deals with the following mental functions:

rhythm
imagination
daydreaming
color
dimension

No matter what you have been taught, somewhere latent within each of you lies each one of these capabilities simply waiting to be freed. Sperry and others also found that the more people use both sides of their brains together, the more the use of each side benefits the other. For example, it was found that the study of music helped the study of mathematics, and the study of mathematics helped the study of music; that the study of rhythm helped the study of languages and that the study of languages helped the learning of bodily rhythms; that the study of dimension helped the study of mathematics and that the study of mathematics helped the brain conceptualize dimension; and so on. It was similarly found that if a person used more of these areas, the more generally capable was his entire memory.

4

The Secret Principles Underlying a Superpower Memory

The Greeks so worshiped memory that they made a goddess out of her—Mnemosyne. It was her name from which was derived the current word *mnemonics,* used to describe memory techniques such as those you are about to learn. In Greek and Roman times, senators would learn these techniques in order to impress other politicians and the public with their phenomenal powers of learning and memory. Using such techniques, the Romans were able to remember, without fault, thousands of items, including statistics relating to their empires. Using these simple but sophisticated techniques, they became the rulers of their time.

Long before we had discovered the physiological breakdown of the functions in the left and right hemispheres of our brains, the Greeks had intuitively realized that there are two underlying principles that ensure perfect memory:

imagination
association

Whereas, in current times, most of us are actively discouraged from using our imaginative abilities, and consequently learn very little about the nature of mental association, the Greeks emphasized these two foundation stones of mental functioning and opened the way for us to develop the techniques even further.

Quite simply, if you want to remember *anything,* all you have to do is to *associate* (link) it with *some known or fixed item* (the memory systems in this book will give you those easily remembered fixed items), calling upon your *imagination* throughout.

The Rules

The rules for perfect memory laid down by the Greeks fit in *exactly* with the information recently discovered about the left and right brains. Without a scientific basis, the Greeks realized that in order to remember well, you have to use every aspect of your mind. In the following five pages I shall outline these rules.

In order to remember well, you must include in your associated and linked mental landscape the following:

1. *Color.* The more colors the merrier, and the more vivid they are, the better. Using color alone can improve your memory by as much as 50 percent.

2. *Imagination.* Your imagination is the powerhouse of your memory. The more vividly you can imagine, the more easily you will remember. Sub-areas within imagination include the following:
   a. Expansion: The more gigantic and enormous you can make your mental images, the better.
   b. Contraction: If you can clearly imagine your picture as extremely tiny, you will remember it well.

c. Absurdity: The more ridiculous, zany, and absurd your mental images are, the more they will be outstanding and thus the more they will be remembered.

3. *Rhythm.* The more rhythm and variation of rhythm in your mental picture, the more that picture will weave itself into your memory.

4. *Movement.* As often as possible, try to make your mental images *move.* Moving objects are usually remembered better than still ones.

5. *The Senses:*
   tasting
   touching
   smelling
   seeing
   hearing

   The more you can involve *all* your senses in your memory image, the more you will remember it. For example, if you have to remember that you have to buy bananas, you stand a far better chance of not forgetting your task if you can actually imagine smelling the banana as you touch it with your hands, bite into it with your mouth and taste it, see it as it is approaching your face, and hear yourself munching it.

6. *Sex.* Sex is one of our strongest drives, and if you apply this aspect of yourself to your magnificent daydreaming ability, your memory will improve.

7. *Sequencing and Ordering.* Imagination alone is not enough for memory. In order to function well, your mind needs order and sequence. This helps it to categorize and structure things in such a way as to make them more easily accessible, much in the same way as an ordered filing system allows easier retrieval of information than if that same information were simply dumped randomly on the floor.

8. *Number*. To make ordering and sequencing easier, it is often advisable to use numbers. Many of the memory systems throughout this book will teach you simple and advanced methods for memorizing using number aids in different ways.
9. *Dimension*. Use your right-brain ability to see your memory images in 3-D.

In each memory system there is a key word. This word is the "key memory word" in that it is the constant peg on which the reader will hang other items he or she wishes to remember. This key memory word is specifically designed to be an "image word" in that it *must* produce a picture or image in the mind of the person using the memory system. Thus the phrase "key memory word image."

As you progress through the increasingly sophisticated mnemonic systems outlined in the following chapters, you will realize the importance of another rule: The pictures you build in your mind must remain basic and associative—i.e., they must contain *only* the items you want to remember, and those items must be associated or connected to key memory images. The connections between your basic memory system images and the things you wish to remember should be as fundamental and uncomplicated as possible.

1. Crashing things together
2. Sticking things together
3. Placing things on top of each other
4. Placing things underneath each other
5. Placing things inside each other
6. Substituting things for each other
7. Placing things in new situations

By now it will be clear to you that the systems worked out by the Greeks and for nearly two thousand years discarded as mere tricks were in fact based on the way in which the human brain actually functions. The ancients realized the importance of words, order, sequence, and number, now known to be functions of the left side of the brain; and of imagination, color, rhythm, dimension, and daydreaming, now known to be right brain functions.

Mnemosyne was to the Greeks the most beautiful of all the goddesses, proved by the fact that Zeus spent more time in her bed than in that of any other goddess or mortal. He slept with her for nine days and nights, and the result of that coupling was the birth of the nine Muses, the goddesses who preside over love poetry, epic poetry, hymns, dance, comedy, tragedy, music, history, and astronomy. For the Greeks, then, the infusion of energy (Zeus) into memory (Mnemosyne) produced both creativity and knowledge.

They were correct. If you apply the mnemonic principles and techniques appropriately, not only will your memory improve in the various areas outlined in this book but your creativity will soar, and with the twin improvements in memory and creativity, your overall mental functioning and assimilation of knowledge will accelerate at the same fantastic pace. In the process you will be developing a new and dynamic synthesis between the left and right side of your brain.

The following chapters take you step by step through first the very simple systems and then the more advanced systems, concluding with the major system, the Star of the Memorizers' Solar System, which will enable you to remember as many *thousands* of items as you wish. In order that you can maintain the extraordinary results that you are going to achieve, a final chapter shows you how to adjust and maintain your memory over a long period of future time.

5

Memory System 1: The Link System

In this chapter you will see for yourself that your memory can improve, and that by improving it, your imaginative powers and your creativity will also be released. The Link System is the most basic of all the memory systems and will give you a foundation with which to make learning the most advanced systems extremely easy. This basic system is used for memorizing short lists of items, such as shopping lists in which each item is linked to or associated with the next. While using this system, you will be using all of these basic Memory Principles:

imagination
association
exaggeration
contraction—making mental images smaller
absurdity—using your sense of the surrealistically ridiculous
    lous
humor
color
rhythm
taste
touch
smell
sight

hearing
sensuality—involving as many of your basic senses as
    possible
sexuality
order and sequence
number
substitution—replacing one image with another—for
    example, the number two with a swan

In using these principles you will be exercising the dynamic relationship between your left and right brain and
thereby increasing the overall power of your brain. Imagine,
for example, that you have been asked to shop for the following items:
    a silver stirring spoon
    six drinking glasses
    bananas
    pure soap
    eggs
    biodegradable washing powder
    dental floss
    wholewheat bread
    tomatoes
    roses

Instead of scrambling around for little bits of paper
(everyone has either done it himself or seen others desperately
fumbling through their pockets for the missing slip) or trying
to remember them all by simple repetition and consequently
forgetting at least two or three, you would simply apply the
basic Memory Principles in the following way:

Imagine yourself walking out your front door perfecting
the most amazing balancing trick: In your mouth is the most
enormous silver-colored serving spoon, the handle-end of
which you are holding between your teeth, as you *taste* and *feel*
the metal in your mouth.

Carefully balanced in the ladle-end of the spoon are six *exaggeratedly* beautiful crystal glasses, through which the sunlight reflects brilliantly into your bedazzled eyes. As you look with delighted amazement at the glasses, you can also *hear* them delicately tinkling on the silver spoon. As you step outside, you step on the most *gigantic yellow* and *brown colored* banana, which skids with a *swish* from under you. Being a fantastic balancer, you barely manage not to fall and confidently place your other foot groundward only to find that you have stepped on a shimmering white bar of pure soap. This being too much for even a master, you fall backward and land seat down on a mound of eggs. As you sink into them, you can *hear* the cracking of the shells, *see* the yellow of the yoke and the white of the albumen, and *sense* the feeling as the dampness sinks into your clothes.

Using your *imaginative* ability to *exaggerate* anything, you speed up time and *imagine,* in a couple of seconds, that you have gone back inside, undressed, washed your soiled clothes in a super biodegradable washing powder, which allows pure, shimmering water to leave the washing machine, and then visualize yourself once again on your way out the front door. This time, because you are slightly tired by the previous accident, you are pulling yourself along toward the shops on a *gigantic* rope made of *millions* of threads of dental floss, the rope *connecting* your front door to the drugstore.

Just as all this exertion and exercise begins to make you feel hungry, wafting on the warm wind comes an *incredibly strong aroma* of freshly baked wholewheat bread. *Imagine* yourself being dragged by the nose as you salivate *extraordinarily* thinking of the *taste* of the freshly baked bread. As you enter the bakery shop, you notice to your amazement that every loaf on the baker's shelves is filled with *brilliantly pulsating red* tomatoes, the baker's latest idea for a new food fad.

As you walk out of the baker's shop, *noisily* munching on your tomato and wholewheat loaf, you see walking down the road with the most amazing *rhythm* the *sexiest* person you have ever seen (really let your imagination go on this one). Your immediate instinct is to buy the person roses, so you dive into the nearest flower shop, which sells nothing but red roses, and buy the lot, *bedazzled* by the *greenness* of the leaves, the *redness* of the flowers, the *feel* of the flowers as you carry them, the *feel* of the thorns, and the *fragrance* from the roses themselves.

When you have finished reading this fantasy, close your eyes and run back through the image-story you have just completed. If you think you can already remember all ten items in the shopping list, turn now to the next page and fill in the answers. If not, read through this chapter again, carefully visualizing on your mind's inner screen, in sequence, the events of the story. Turn to the next page when you are ready.

Memory Test

Note here the ten items you had to buy.

spoon
Bannanas
glasses
flos
eggs
tomatoe
Bread
roses

If you scored seven or more, you are already in the top 1 percent of scores for the memorization of such a list. And you have now used the basic keys for unlocking much of the limitless potential of your brain.

Practice the Link System on a couple of lists of your own devising, making sure that you use the basic Memory Principles throughout, remembering that the *more* imaginative, absurd, and sensual you can be, the better. When you have had a little practice with the Link System, move on to the next chapter.

6

Memory System 2: The Number-Shape System

In Chapter 5 you learned the right-brained Link System, in which you applied all the basic Memory Principles with the exception of number and order. We now move on to the first of the Peg Memory Systems. A Peg Memory System differs from the Link System only in that it uses a special list of Key Memory Images that never change and to which everything that you wish to remember can be linked and associated. A Peg System can be thought of much like a clothes cabinet containing a certain definite number of hangers on which you hang your clothes. The hangers themselves never change, but the clothes that are hung on them vary infinitely. In the Number-Shape System, which is the first of the Peg Systems we'll cover, the number and shape represent the hangers, and the things you wish to remember with the system represent the clothes to be hung on the hangers. The system is an easy one and uses only the numbers from 1 to 10.

The best system is one you will create yourself—rather than one supplied by me. This is because every mind is infinitely varied, and the associations, links, and images that you may have will generally be different from mine and everyone else's. The associations and images you generate from your own creative imagination will last far longer and be much more effective than any that could be "implanted." I shall therefore explain exactly how you can construct a system and then I'll give examples of its practical use.

In the Number-Shape System, all you have to do is think of images for each of the numbers from 1 to 10, each image reminding you of the number because both the image and the number have the same shape. For example, and to make your task a little easier, the key memory-shape word that most people use for the number 2 is the Swan because the number 2 is shaped like a swan, and similarly because a swan looks like a living, elegant version of the number 2.

In the Number-Shape System, images that "look like" the number are used as hangers, or hooks, on which to link items you wish to remember. For example, a common Key Image for the number 2 is a swan.

On pages 54 and 55 are listed the numbers from 1 to 10, with a blank beside each number for you to pencil in the various words that you think *best* image the shape of the numbers. As you select the words, try to make sure that they are exceptionally good *visual* images, with lots of good color and basic imagination-potential within them. They should be images to which you will be able to link the things you wish to remember with ease and enjoyment.

Here are several examples:

1 Pole, pencil, pen, penis, straw, candle
2 Swan, duck, goose
3 Breasts, double chin, behind, molehills
4 Sailing boat, table, chair
5 Cymbal and drum, hook, pregnant woman
6 Elephant's trunk, golf club, cherry, pipe
7 Cliff, fishing line, flag, boomerang
8 Bun, snowman, hourglass, shapely woman
9 Tennis racquet, sperm, tadpole, lorgnette
10 Bat and ball, Laurel and Hardy

Give yourself not more than ten minutes to complete the list from 1 to 10, and even if you find some numbers difficult, don't worry; just read on.

NUMBER	NUMBER SHAPE MEMORY WORDS
1	
2	
3	
4	
5	

6

7

8

9

10

Now that you have generated several of your own number-images and have seen other suggestions, you should select the Number-Shape Key Memory *Image* for each number that is the best one for you.

When you have done this, turn to page 56 and draw in your appropriate image for each number. (Don't feel inhibited if you consider yourself not good at art; your right brain needs the practice.) The more colors you can use in your images, the better.

At the end of this paragraph you should close your eyes and test yourself by mentally running through the numbers from 1 to 10 in order. As you come to each number, mentally link it with the Number-Shape Key Memory Image you have selected and drawn, using the basic Memory Principles throughout, especially exaggeration, color, and movement. Make sure you actually *see* the images on the videoscreen of your closed eyelids. When you have done this exercise once, run through the numbers in reverse order, again linking them with your chosen word and again applying the basic Memory Principles. Next, pick out numbers randomly and as quickly as you can, making a game to see how quickly the image comes to mind. And finally reverse the whole process by flashing the images on your internal videoscreen, seeing how quickly you can connect the basic numbers to your images. Do this exercise now.

NUMBER	NUMBER-SHAPE IMAGE
1	
2	
3	
4	
5	
6	
7	
8	
9	
10	

If you managed to do this successfully, you have already accomplished a memory feat that most people would find difficult if not impossible. You have now forged into your memory and creative imagination a system that you will be able to use throughout your life and that combines both the qualities of the left and the right hemispheres of your brain.

The use of the system is simple and enjoyable and involves the other major memory device: linking/association. For example, if you have a list of ten items that you wish to remember not simply by linking, as in the previous chapter, but in numerical order, reverse numerical order, and random numerical order, the Number-Shape System makes the whole process easy. Let us put it to the test:

Assume you have been asked to remember the following list of items:

1. A symphony

2. Prayer

3. Watermelon

4. Volcano

5. Motorcycle

6. Sunshine

7. Apple pie

8. Blossoms

9. Space shuttle

10. Field of wheat

To remember these items in *any* order, all that you have to do is to link them with the appropriate Number-Shape Key Memory Image. As with the Link System, and all memory systems, the basic Memory Principles should be applied throughout; the more imaginative you can be, the better. Give yourself not more than three minutes to complete your memorization of these ten items, using the Number-Shape System, and then test yourself by filling in the answers on this page. If you feel confident, start this exercise now; if not, read the examples given on page 54, and then turn back to this page to fill in the answers.

Fill in both your Number-Shape Image Word and the words you were asked to remember with each number.

Number-Shape System

Link-Test Items	Key Number-Shape Image	Item Test Memorizer
10	9	1
9	7	2
8	5	3
7	3	4
6	1	5
5	2	6
4	4	7
3	6	8
2	10	9
1	8	10
Score out of <u>10</u>		Total score out of <u>30</u>

Cover your first answers and complete the second test.

Cover your answers and complete the final test.

As a guide for those who might have had a little difficulty with this exercise, the following are examples of possible ways in which the ten items to be memorized might have been linked to the Number-Shape Key Memory Images:

1. For symphony you might have imagined a conductor conducting frantically with a gigantic pole or pencil, knocking over most of the musicians as he did so, with ensuing pandemonium; or you might have

imagined all the violinists playing their instruments with straws; or again you might have imagined them all with gigantic penises. Whatever your image, the basic Memory Principles should be applied.

2. Prayer is an abstract word. It is often mistakenly assumed that abstract words are hard to memorize. Using proper memory techniques, you will find that this is not the case, as you may have already discovered. All you have to do is to "image" the abstract in concrete form. In this instance you might have imagined your swan or duck or goose with its wings upheld like hands in prayer; or filled an imaginary church with imaginary swans, geese, or ducks being led in a prayer service by a minister who was also a bird.

3. Easy!

4. You might have imagined your gigantic volcano within the ocean, seeing it erupting red and furiously beneath your yacht, the steam and hissing created by the volcano actually heaving your yacht right off the water; or you might have had your volcano miniaturized and placed on a chair on which you were about to sit (you would certainly *feel* it); or imagined a mountainous table actually blocking the power of the volcano.

5. A giant hook might have come down from the sky and lifted you and your motorcycle off the road along which you were speeding; or you on your motorcycle might have crashed, incredibly noisily and disruptively, into a drum shop; or seated astride the motorcycle is the most enormous pregnant woman you have ever seen.

6. Sunshine could be pouring out of your pipe; or you might have flung the golf club rhythmically up into

the air, and it got entangled in a sunbeam and drawn toward the sun; or the sunbeam could be zapping like a lazer into a cherry, making it grow gigantic before your very eyes, as you imagine the taste as you bite into it, the juices dribbling down your chin.

7. Your gigantic cliff could actually be made entirely of apple pie; or your fishing line could catch, instead of a fish, a bedraggled, soggy but nevertheless still scrumptious apple pie; or your boomerang could fly off into the distance and, with a *thunk,* end up in an apple pie as big as a mountain, not returning to you but sending only the delicious smells of the apple and the piecrust.

8. Your snowman could be decorated entirely with exquisitely pink blossoms; or your hourglass could tell the time not by the falling of sand but by the gentle falling of millions of tiny blossoms within the hourglass (see illustration); or your shapely woman could be walking provocatively through endless fields of waist-high fallen blossoms.

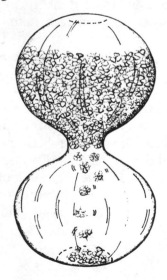

9. You could miniaturize your space shuttle and make it into one of thousands of tadpoles; or miniaturize it even further and have it as the leading sperm about to fertilize an egg; or imagine it leaving Earth's atmosphere with a flag as big as the moon on its nose.

10. You feel the shock in your bat as it cracks against the ball, and you see the ball sailing across endless fields of rhythmically waving, beautifully golden wheat; or you image Laurel and Hardy playing the ultimate fools and thrashing around, while trampling, the same endless fields of wheat.

These are, of course, only examples, and are included to indicate the kind of exaggeration, imagination, sensuality, and creative thinking that is necessary to establish the most effective memory links. As with the Link System, it is essential that you practice this system on your own. I recommend giving yourself at least one test before you move to the next chapter.

One of the best ways to do this is to check yourself with members of your family or with friends. Ask them to make up a list of any ten items and to read the list to you with about a 5- to 10-second pause between each item. The instant they have given you the item to be memorized, make the most wild, colorful, exaggerated associations possible, projecting images onto your internal screen, and thus consolidating them as you progress.

You (and they) will be amazed at the ease with which you can remember the items, and it is most impressive when you are able to repeat them in reverse and random order.

Don't worry about confusing previous lists of items with new ones. As I mentioned at the beginning of the chapter, this particular Peg System can be compared to coat hangers—you simply remove one coat (association) and replace it with another.

In the next chapter I shall introduce a second system based on the numbers one to ten: the Number-Rhyme System. These two systems can then be combined to enable you to remember twenty items with as much facility as you have just remembered ten. In subsequent chapters more sophisticated systems will be introduced to allow you to store lists of items stretching into the thousands. These systems are recommended for long-term memory, the things you wish to retain over a long period of time. The Number-Shape System you have just learned and the Number-Rhyme System you are about to learn are recommended for your short-term memory purposes—those items you wish to remember for only a few hours.

Give yourself about a day to become skilled in using the techniques you have learned so far before moving to the next chapter.

7

Memory System 3: The Number-Rhyme System

You will find the Number-Rhyme System especially easy to learn, since it is identical in principle to the Number-Shape System. Also, like the Number-Shape System, it can be used for remembering short lists of items that you need to store in your memory for only a brief time. In this system, as before, use the numbers from 1 to 10, and instead of having Key Memory Images that resemble the shape of the number, you devise Key Memory Images represented by a word that *rhymes* with the sound of the number. For example, the Key Rhyming Memory Image Word that most people use for the number 5 is "hive," the images that they use ranging from one enormous hive from which emanates a sky-covering swarm of monster bees to a microscopic hive with only one tiny bee.

As with the Link System and the Number-Rhyme System, it is essential to apply the basic Memory Principles, making each image as imaginative, colorful, and sensual as you possibly can. As in the previous chapter, you will find listed the numbers from 1 to 10, with a blank beside each for you to pencil in the Rhyming Image Word that you think will produce the best image for each number. Make sure that the images will be good memory hooks for you.

By now your associative and creative thinking abilities will have already improved your mental capacity, so give yourself not five minutes as before but three minutes to fill in your initial Key Image Words:

NUMBER	NUMBER-SOUND MEMORY WORD
1	
2	
3	
4	
5	
6	
7	
8	
9	
10	

As before, I am going to offer a few alternative image-ideas commonly used. Consider these and your own Key Rhyming Word Images, and select for each number, from 1 to 10, the one you consider to be best for you.

Some popular choices:

1. Sun, bun, nun, hun, gun
2. Shoe, pew, loo, crew, gnu
3. Tree, flea, sea, knee, me
4. Door, moor, whore, boar, maw
5. Hive, jive, drive, dive, chive
6. Sticks, pricks, bricks, wicks, hicks
7. Heaven, Devon
8. Bait, gate, weight, date, fate
9. Vine, wine, twine, line, dine
10. Hen, pen, den, wren, men

Now select the most appropriate Key Rhyming Image Word and, as in the previous chapter, draw your image, using as much imagination and color as possible, in the space provided on the following page.

Number Rhyme Images

NUMBER	NUMBER RHYME KEY IMAGE
1	
2	
3	
4	
5	
6	
7	
8	
9	
10	

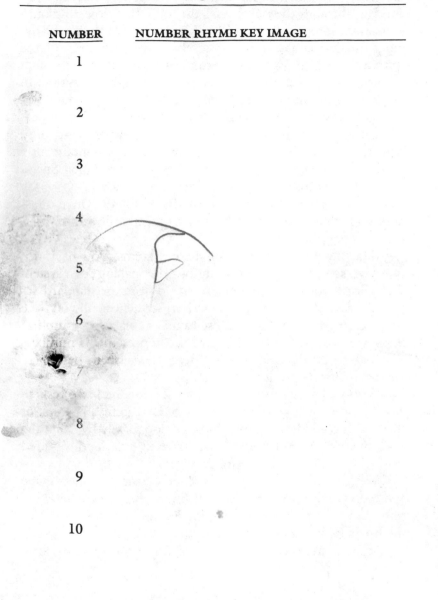

After you have finished reading this paragraph, test yourself with your chosen Key Rhyming Image. Close your eyes, and run through the numbers 1 through 10, projecting onto your inner screen a clear and brilliant picture of the Key Rhyming Image you have for each number. First, run through the system from 1 to 10 in the normal order; next, run through the system in reverse order; next, run through the system in random order; finally, pick the images "out of the air," and connect the numbers to them. As you do each exercise, repeat it, making each repetition faster than the previous one, until you acquire such skill that your mind will instantaneously produce the image as soon as you think of the number. Spend at least five minutes on this exercise, starting now.

Now that you have mastered the Number-Rhyme System, you will see that it can be used in exactly the same way as the Number-Shape System.

Having mastered both of these systems, you have not only two separate 1 to 10 systems but the makings of a system that allows you to remember *twenty* objects in standard sequence, reverse sequence, and random sequence. All you have to do is to establish one of these two systems as the numbers from 1 to 10, letting the other system represent the numbers from 11 to 20. Decide which system you wish to be which, and immediately put it to the test!

You will remember that chapter 2 contained two tests in which you were asked to remember twenty items. The first of these tests could have been completed adequately by using the Link System, but the second was more difficult and required some form of basic Peg Memory System.

Let us then apply our knowledge of the Number-Shape and Number-Rhyme systems to the more difficult of these two tests. Give yourself approximately five minutes to memorize the list, which is repeated at the end of this paragraph. When your time is up, turn to page 71 and fill in the answers. Start now:

1. Atom
2. Tree
3. Stethoscope
4. Sofa
5. Alley
6. Tile
7. Windscreen
8. Honey
9. Brush
10. Toothpaste
11. Glitter
12. Heater
13. Railway
14. Lighter
15. Wart
16. Star
17. Peace
18. Button
19. Pram
20. Pump

Number-Shape and Number-Rhyme Memory Test

Opposite are three columns of twenty numbers: The first in standard order; the second in reverse order; the third in random order. Complete each list filling in, next to the number, the appropriate word from the list you have just memorized, covering the lists with your hand or with paper as you complete them and start on the next. When you have finished, examine your score out of a possible sixty points.

1	20	11
2	19	15
3	18	10
4	17	3
5	16	17
6	15	20
7	14	4
8	13	9
9	12	5
10	11	19
11	10	8
12	9	13
13	8	1
14	7	18
15	6	7
16	5	16
17	4	6
18	3	12
19	2	2
20	1	14

Score, out of 60 points:_____

You will almost certainly have made an improvement over your performance in the original test, but you might find that you are still having difficulty with certain associations. Check any such "weak" associations and examine the reasons for any failure. These reasons usually include: not enough exaggeration and imagination; not enough color; not enough movement; weak links; not enough sensuality; and not enough humor. Take confidence from the fact that the more you practice, the more such weak links will become a matter of history. Today and tomorrow test yourself whenever possible. Ask as many of your friends and acquaintances as possible to try to catch you out on lists that they make up for you to remember.

On the first few attempts, you will undoubtedly make some errors, but even so, you will be performing far beyond the average. Consider any errors and mistakes you make to be good opportunities for examining—and subsequently strengthening—any areas of weakness in your memory systems and the way you apply them. If you persevere, you will soon be able to fire back lists given to you without any hesitation and without any fear of failure. You will then be able to use the systems confidently—for pleasure, for entertainment, for practical use, and for exercising your general memory.

As you become more skilled, keep a continuing and growing list of the areas in your life in which you will apply the systems you are currently learning. The blank pages at the back of the book have been provided for you to keep a record of the areas in which you are going to apply the systems.

In the next chapter you will learn the basic system used and developed by the first recorded masters of mnemonics, the Romans.

8

Memory System 4: The Roman Room System

The Romans were great inventors and practitioners of mnemonic techniques, one of their most popular being the Roman Room. The Romans constructed such a system easily. They imagined the entrance to their house and their room and then filled the room with as many objects and items of furniture as they chose—each object and piece of furniture serving as a link-image onto which they attached the things they wished to remember. The Romans were particularly careful not to make a mental garbage dump of their room; precision and order (attributes of the left side of your brain) are essential in this system.

A Roman might, for example, have constructed his imaginary entrance and room with two gigantic pillars at either side of the front door, a symbol of a lion as his door-knob, and an exquisite Greek statue on the immediate left as he walked in. Next to the statue might have been a flowering plant; next to the plant, a large sofa covered with the fur of one of the animals the subject had hunted; and, in front of the sofa, a large marble table on which were placed goblets, a wine container, bowls of fruit, and so forth.

Let's say that the Roman then wished to remember to buy a pair of sandals, to get his sword sharpened, to buy a new servant, to tend to his grapevine, to polish his helmet, to talk to his child, and so on. He would simply imagine the first pillar at the entrance of his imaginary room festooned with thousands of sandals, the leather polished and glistening, and the smell delighting his nostrils; on the right-hand pillar he would imagine sharpening his sword on the pillar itself, hearing the scraping as he did so, noticing the dust falling to the ground, and feeling the blade as it became sharper and sharper; his servant he would imagine riding a roaring lion, while grapes he might remember by imagining his exquisite statue totally entwined with a grapevine on which were luscious grapes that he could imagine seeing and tasting so well that he would actually salivate; his helmet he could imagine by substituting the container of his imaginary flowers with the helmet itself, having some of the blooms actually protruding through the various spaces in his helmet; finally, he could imagine himself on his sofa, his arm around the child to whom he wished to speak.

The Roman Room System is particularly amenable to the use of the left and right brain, and to the Memory Principles, because it requires very precise structuring and ordering, as well as a lot of imagination and sensuality. The delight of this system is that the room is *entirely* imaginary, so you can have in it every wonderful item that you wish: things that please all your senses, items of furniture and objects of art you have always desired to possess in real life, and similarly foods and decorations that especially appeal to you. Another major advantage of using this system is that if you begin to imagine yourself in possession of certain items that exist in your imaginary room, both your memory and creative intelligence will begin to work subconsciously on ways in which you can actually acquire such objects, increasing the probability that you will eventually do so.

The Roman Room System eliminates all boundaries on your imagination and allows you to remember as many items as you wish: All you have to do is make the room as large, as many-walled, and as full of objects as you wish. On page 76 there is space for you to jot down quickly your first thoughts on the items you would like to have in your room, the shape and design of your room, and so on. When you have completed this, turn to pages 76 and 77, draw your ideal Memory Room, either as an artist's drawing or as an architect's plan, both drawing and printing in the names of items with which you are going to furnish and decorate it. Many people find this to be their favorite memory system, and they use enormous sheets of paper on which they include hundreds of items in a gigantic room. If you wish to do this, by all means do so.

When you have completed this task, take a number of "mental walks" around your room, memorizing precisely the order, position, and number of items in the room (left brain) and similarly sensing with *all* of your senses the colors, tastes, feels, smells, and sounds within your room.

As with the previous memory systems you have learned, practice memorizing using the Roman Room System both alone and with friends, until the system is a firmly established technique.

Roman

Room

Initial Roman-Room Thoughts

9

Memory System 5:
The Alphabet System

The Alphabet System is the final Peg System and is similar in construction to the Number-Shape and Number-Rhyme systems, the only difference being that instead of using numbers, it uses the twenty-six letters of the alphabet. As with all the other memory systems, the basic Memory Principles apply. The rules for constructing your Alphabet Memory System are simple; they are as follows: You select a Key Memory Image Word that starts with the sound of the letter and is easily memorized. If you think of several possibilities for a letter, use the one that comes first in the dictionary. For example, for the letter *L* it would be possible to use *el*astic, *el*egy, *el*ephant, *el*bow, *el*m, etc. If you were looking up these words in the dictionary, the first one you would come to would be *el*astic, and that is therefore the word you would select for your Alphabet System. The reason for this rule is that if you should ever forget your Alphabet Key Word Image, you can mentally flick through the letters of the alphabet in order, rapidly arriving at the correct word. In the example given, if you had forgotten your Alphabet System image for the letter *L*, you would try *ela* and would immediately be able to recall your Key Image Word, *elastic*.

Another rule in the construction of your Alphabet System is that if the letter itself makes a word (for example *I* makes the word *eye*, and *J* makes the word *jay*, the bird), then that word should be used. In some cases, it is possible to use meaningful initials instead of complete words—for example, UN.

On page 81 are listed the letters of the alphabet. Paying close attention to the now-familiar rules for constructing a system, pencil in your own Alphabet System Image Word.

LETTER	ALPHABET MEMORY WORD
A	
B	
C	
D	
E	
F	
G	
H	
I	
J	
K	
L	
M	
N	
O	
P	
Q	
R	
S	
T	
U	
V	
W	
X	
Y	
Z	

Now that you have completed your initial thoughts, re-check the Alphabet Image Words, making sure you have started your words with the *sound* of the letter or letter-word and not simply the letter itself. For example, *ant, bottle, case, dogs,* and *eddy* would not be correct Alphabet System Image Words because they do not start with the *sound* of the letter as it is pronounced when you are reciting the alphabet. Having rechecked your own words, now compare them with the following list of suggestions, and when you have done so, select your final list.

A   Ace (those of you with knowledge of American history might use Abe)

B   Bee (the letter makes a word; this is the word that should be used in all cases)

C   Sea (the same rule applies)

D   Deed (legal, though the initials DDT may be preferred)

E   Easel

F   Effervesce

G   Jean (or "Gee!")

H   H-bomb

I   Eye

J   Jay

K   Cake

L   Elastic (or *elbow,* if you pronounce *elastic* with a long *e*)

M   MC (emcee)

N   Enamel (or *entire,* if you pronounce *enamel* with a long *e*)

O   Oboe

P   Pea (first alphabetically!)

Q   Queue

R   Arch

S   Eskimo

T   Tea (or perhaps T-square)

U   U-boat (*you* is too vague)

V   Vehicle (or the initials VD)

W   WC

X   X-ray

Y   Wife

Z   Zebra

Now make your final choices and draw your images on the following pages.

Final Alphabet Memory Key Word Image

LETTER	ALPHABET MEMORY WORD IMAGE
A	
B	
C	
D	
E	
F	
G	
H	
I	
J	
K	
L	

M

N

O

P

Q

R

S

T

U

V

W

X

Y

Z

When you have completed your Alphabet Memory Key Word Images, review them in exactly the same way as with the previous memory systems, mentally visualizing them in standard order, reverse order, and random order. Similarly, make sure you test the system individually, and then with family or friends.

Now you have learned the introductory, basic Link and Peg Memory systems. From now on, apart from a brief summary of these concepts in the next chapter, you will be learning more advanced, expansive, and sophisticated systems that will enable you to remember dates, jokes, languages, examinations, names and faces, books, dreams, and lists of *hundreds,* even *thousands* of items.

10

How to Increase by 100 Percent Everything You Have Learned So Far

You have now completed the five individual Memory Systems: Link, Number-Shape, Number-Rhyme, Roman Room, and Alphabet systems. Each of these systems can be used either independently or in conjunction with another system. Furthermore, one or two of the systems can be set aside, if you wish, as "constant memory banks." That is, if you have certain lists or orders of items that you will need to be able to recall over a period of a year or more, you can set aside the system of your choice for this purpose.

Before moving on to the broader systems, however, I want to introduce you to a simple and intriguing method for instantly doubling the capacity of any of the systems you have learned so far. When you have reached the end of a system but wish to add further associations, all you have to do is to go back to the beginning of your system and imagine your association word exactly as you usually imagine it, but as if it were contained in a huge block of ice. This simple visualization technique will drastically change the association pictures you have formed and will double the effectiveness of your system by giving you the original list plus that list in its new context.

For example, if your first key in the Number-Shape System was *telephone pole,* you would imagine that same telephone pole either buried in the heart of your giant block of ice or protruding from the corners or sides. If your first word in the Number-Rhyme System was *sun,* then you could imagine its fierce rays melting the edges of the ice block in which it was contained. If your first word in the Alphabet System was *Ace,* then you could imagine a giant playing card either frozen in the center or forming one of the six sides of the ice block. If, therefore, you were using your "second" Alphabet system, (the alphabet in a huge block of ice), and the first item you wanted to remember was *parrot,* you might imagine your parrot crashing through the center heart, spade, club, or diamond of your card, shattering, with lots of squawking, and cracking, the block of ice.

You now have the ability to remember randomly linked items, two sets of ten items, a large number of ordered items (your Roman Room), and twenty-six ordered items. And you can instantly double that capacity by using the "block of ice" method. Having reached this stage and having by now enormously increased the flexibility of your mind, your abilities to imagine, associate, sense, and create are ready to take on and easily master the grandfather of all the systems: the Major System, a system that can be used to create—should you so wish—*limitless* memory systems!

11

The Major System

The Major System is the ultimate Memory System. It has been used and continually improved upon for more than three hundred years, since the middle of the seventeenth century, when it was introduced by Stanislaus Mink von Wennsshein. Von Wennsshein's basic construction was modified in the early eighteenth century by Dr. Richard Grey, an Englishman. The Major System was devised to enable the master memorizers of the time to break the bonds of the previously excellent but more limited systems. These master memorizers wanted a system that would enable them to memorize a list of items not only longer than ten but as long as they wanted. At the same time they wanted this system to enable them to remember numbers and dates and to enable them to order and structure memory in hundreds and thousands of detailed ways.

The basic concept of the system is that it makes use of a different consonant or consonant sound for each number from 0 through 9 in a special code:

The Major System's Special Code

0 = s, z, soft c

1 = d, t, th

2 = n

3 = m

4 = r

5 = l

6 = j, sh, ch, dg, soft g

7 = k, ch, hard c, hard g, ng, q

8 = f, v

9 = b, p

10 = s, z, soft c

The vowels *a, e, i, o, u* and the letters *h, w,* and *y* do not have numbers associated with them and are used simply as "blanks" in the Key Memory Word Images you will soon be creating.

To save you the trouble of remembering these by rote, there are some simple remembering devices:

1. The letters *d* and *t* have one downstroke.

2. The letter *n* has two downstrokes.

3. The letter *m* has three downstrokes.

4. The letter *r* is the last letter in the word *four*.

5. The letter *l* can be thought of as either the Roman numeral for 50 or the shape of a spread hand with five spread fingers.

6. The letter *j* is the mirror image of 6.

7. The letter *k*, when seen as a capital, contains two number 7s.

8. The letter *f*, when written, has two loops; similar to the number 8.

9. The letters *b* and *p* are the mirror image of 9.

10. The letter *s*, or z, is the first sound of the word *zero; o* is the last letter.

As with the Number-Rhyme and Number-Shape systems, your task is to create a Key Word Image that can be immediately and permanently linked with the number it represents. Take, for example, the number 1. You have to think of a Key Image Word that is a good visual image and that contains only *t, d,* or *th* and a vowel sound. Examples include *tea, toe, doe,* and *the*. When recalling the word chosen for number 1, let us say *doe,* you would know that it could represent only the number 1 because the consonant letters in the word represent no other number, and vowels do not count as numbers in our system.

Try another example: the number 34. In this case the number three is represented by the letter *m*, and 4 is represented by the letter *r*. Examples of possible words include *mare, more, moor,* and *mire*. In selecting the "best" word for this number, you once again make use of the alphabet-order to assist both in choice of word and in recall: In other words, the letters you have to choose are *m* and *r*, so you simply mentally run through the vowels *a-e-i-o-u* using the *first* vowel that enables you to make an adequate Memory Word. The case in question is easily solved, since *a* fits between *m* and *r* to direct you toward the word *mare*.

The advantage of using this alphabet-order system is that, should a word in the Major System ever be forgotten, it can actually be "worked out" from the basic information. All you have to do is place the letters of the number in their correct order and then "slot in," in order, the vowels. As soon as you touch the correct combination, your key Memory Word Image will immediately come to mind.

First, letting the letter *d* represent in each case the "1" of the number, try to complete the words for numbers 10 to 19, using the alphabet-order system for these numbers. Use page 93, Initial Major System Exercise.

Don't worry if this exercise proves a little difficult, because immediately following is a complete list of Memory Words for the numbers 1 to 100. Don't just accept them: Check each one carefully, changing any that you find difficult to visualize or for which you have a better substitute.

Initial Major System Exercise

10

11

12

13

14

15

16

17

18

19

You now possess the code and keys to a Peg Memory System for the numbers from 1 to 100—a system that contains the pattern for its own memorization. As you have seen, this system is basically limitless. In other words, now that you have letters for the numbers 0 through 9, it should be possible for you to devise Key Word Images for the numbers not only from 1 to 100 but also from 100 to 1,000. This system could of course go on forever.

On the pages that follow I have devised a list of Key Word Images for the numbers 100 to 1,000. After certain of the more difficult words I have included: (1) a suggestion for a way in which an image might be formed from the word; or

(2) a dictionary definition of the word, the definition including words or ideas that should help you form your image; or (3) "new" definitions for words that place them in a humorous or unusual but certainly more memorable form.

The remaining words are followed by blank spaces. In the space provided you should write in your own Key Words for, or ideas about, the image you will be using. In some cases, where the combination of letters makes the use of single words impossible, double words have been used, such as "no cash" for the number 276 (*n*, hard *c*, *sh*). In other cases it is necessary to include vowels (which have no numerical meaning) at the beginning of the word. For example, the number 394 (*m*, *p*, *r*) is represented by the word *empire*. In still other cases, words have been used, the first three letters only of which pertain to the number. For example, the number 359 (*m*, *l*, *b*) is represented by the word *mailbag*. The final *g* is ignored.

If you wish to expand your Major System beyond 100, your next task is to check this Major System list carefully. It would obviously be too much to ask you to do this at one sitting, so I suggest the more modest goal of checking, making images for, and remembering, a hundred items each day. As you go through the list, make every effort to make your images of the words as solid as you can. Remember that as you memorize this entire list, you should try to use both sides of your brain, making sure that you are reviewing and consolidating the order, while at the same time increasing and expanding your imagination, your creativity, and your awareness of your senses. Enough space has been left in this book for you to sketch images if you wish, while you are memorizing your basic list.

1	Tea	26	Nash
2	Noah	27	Nag
3	Ma	28	Navy
4	Ray	29	Nab
5	Law	30	Mace
6	Jaw	31	Mat
7	Key	32	Man
8	Foe	33	Mama
9	Pa	34	Mare
10	Daze	35	Mail
11	Dad	36	Mash
12	Dan	37	Mac
13	Dam	38	Mafia
14	Dare	39	Map
15	Dale	40	Race
16	Dash	41	Rat
17	Deck	42	Rain
18	Dave	43	Ram
19	Dab	44	Rare
20	NASA	45	Rail
21	Net	46	Rash
22	Nan	47	Rack
23	Name	48	Rafia
24	Nero	49	Rape
25	Nail	50	Lace

51	Lad	76	Cash
52	Lane	77	Cake
53	Lamb	78	Café
54	Lair	79	Cab
55	Lily	80	Face
56	Lash	81	Fat
57	Lake	82	Fan
58	Laugh	83	Fame
59	Lab	84	Far
60	Chase	85	Fall
61	Chat	86	Fish
62	Chain	87	Fake
63	Chime	88	Fife
64	Chair	89	Fab
65	Chill	90	Base
66	Cha-cha	91	Bat
67	Check	92	Ban
68	Chaff	93	Bam!
69	Chap	94	Bar
70	Case	95	Ball
71	Cat	96	Bash
72	Can	97	Back
73	Camshaft	98	Beef
74	Car	99	Baby
75	Call	100	Disease

Even when words refer to ideas or concepts, bring them down to a more concrete level. For example, the number 368, represented by the Memory Words *much force* should not be pictured as some vague power or energy in space but should be visualized as an image in which much force is used to accomplish or destroy—for example, a weight lifter at the Olympics. In other words, in each case you will be attempting to make the Memory Word as pictorial and as memorable as possible. Remember the rules in the early chapter: exaggerate; move; substitute; be absurd.

In cases where words are similar in concept to previous words, it is most important to make your images as different as possible. The same caution applies to words that are pluralized because of the addition of *s*. In these cases, imagine a great number of items as opposed to one enormous item. You will find your consolidation of the words in the Major System useful not only because it will enable you to remember the astounding number of 1,000 items (in order or randomly) but also because it will exercise your creative linking ability, which is so necessary for remembering anything.

A number of the words used as mnemonics in this Major System are interesting in their own right. As you check through and memorize each list of 100, have a dictionary by your side, for help if you run into difficulty selecting your Key Words. In these instances, it will serve as a means of solidifying the images for you, will enable you to select the best possible images or words, and will be of value in the improvement of your general vocabulary. If you have read my book *Speed Reading,* combine, where feasible, the vocabulary exercises included in it with your exercises on the Major System.

100 Daisies

101 Dust

102 Design

103 Dismay

104 Desert

105 Dazzle

106 Discharge

107 Disc

108 Deceive

109 Despair

110 Dates—succulent, sticky fruit, often eaten at Christmas

111 Deadwood—decayed, often twisted remains of trees

112 Deaden

113 Diadem—a crown; a wreath of leaves or flowers worn around the head

114 Daughter

115 Detail

116 Detach

117 Toothache

118 Dative—A noun case that expresses giving

119 Deathbed

120 Tennis

121 Dent

122 Denun—To take a nun or nuns away from a place or situation

123 Denim

124 Dinner

125 Downhill

126 Danish—native to Denmark; like the Great Dane dog

127 Dank—unpleasantly soaked or damp; marshy or swampy

128 Downfall

129 Danube—the river (or picture waltzing to the Blue Danube)

130 Demise—the death of a sovereign

131 Domed—having a large, rounded summit, as a head or a church

132 Demon

133 Demimonde—the fringe of society

134 Demure

135 Dimly

136 Damage

137 Democracy

138 Dam Full

139 Damp

140 Dress

141 Dart

142 Drain

143 Dram

144 Drawer

145 Drill

146 Dredge—apparatus for bringing up mud (or oysters) from the sea or river bottom

147 Drag

148 Drive

149 Drip

150 Deluxe

151 Daylight

152 Delinquent

153 Dilemma—a position leaving a choice that is usually between two evils

154 Dealer

155 Delilah—temptress of Samson; false and wily woman

156 Deluge—a great flood; Noah's flood

157 Delicacy

158 Delphi—the ancient Greek town where the sanctuary of the oracle was located

159 Tulip

160 Duchess

161 Dashed

162 Dudgeon—state of strong anger, resentment, or feeling of offense

163 Dutchman

164 Dodger—a wily, tricky, elusive person

165 Dash light—imagine the dash light in your car

166 Dishwasher—abbreviation for dishwashing machine

167 Dechoke—Reverse the image of choke, either in relation to a car or to strangling someone

168 Dishevel—to make the hair or clothes loose, disordered, "flung about"

169 Dish-up—to serve food, usually applied to a slapdash manner

170 Decks

171 Decade

172 Token

173 Decamp—Imagine confusion in the dismantling of tents, etc.

174 Decree—an order made by an authority demanding some kind of action.

175 Ducal—imagine anything similar to or looking like a duke

176 Duckish

177 Decaying

178 Takeoff

179 Decapitate

180 Deface

181 Defeat

182 Divan

183 Defame

184 Diver

185 Defile

186 Devotion

187 Defeat

188 Two frisky fillies—imagine them in a field or memorable enclosure

189 Two frightened boys—perhaps being chased by 188!

190 Debase—to lower in character, quality, or value

191 Debate

192 Debone—to pick the bones out of, usually from fish

193 Whitebeam—a tree with long, silvery underleaves

194 Dipper—imagine the Big Dipper star constellation

195 Dabble

196 Debauch

197 Dipping—imagine someone being dipped forcibly into water, as the medieval torture

198 Dab off—imagine a stain or blood being "dabbed off" with cotton wool

199 Depip—to take the pips out of (imagine a pomegranate)

200 Nieces

201 Nosed—sniffed or smelled out, often applied to hunting animals

202 Insane

203 Noisome—harmful, noxious, ill-smelling

204 No Sir!

205 Nestle

206 Incision—a clean cutting of something, as with a doctor's scalpel

207 Nosegay—a small bunch of sweet-scented flowers

208 Unsafe

209 Newsboy

210 Notice

211 Needed

212 Indian

213 Anatomy

214 Nadir—the lowest point; place or time of great depression

215 Needle

216 Night watch

217 Antique

218 Native

219 Nitboy—a boy who is always doing addleheaded things

220 Ninnies—group of people with weak minds; simpletons

221 Ninth—imagine the ninth hole of a golf course

222 Ninon—a lightweight dress fabric made of silk

223 No name—imagine a person who has forgotten his name

224 Nunnery

225 Union hall

226 Nunish—pertaining to or like a nun

227 Non-aqua—having nothing at all to do with water

228 Nineveh

229 Ninepin—one of nine upright pieces of wood to be knocked down in the game of ninepins

230 Names

231 Nomad

232 Nominee—a person nominated for a position or office

233 No ma'am

234 Enamor—to bring to life, to animate with love

235 Animal

236 No mash—imagine a saucepan that has just been emptied of mashed potatoes

237 Unmake

238 Nymph—a beautiful, mythological maiden, always young

239 Numb

240 Nurse

241 Narrate

242 No run

243 Norm—a standard; a set pattern to be maintained

244 Narrower

245 Nearly

246 Nourish

247 New York

248 Nerve

249 Nearby

250 Nails

251 Nailed

252 Nylon

253 New loam—freshly turned rich and fertile soil

254 Kneeler

255 Nail hole

256 Knowledge

257 Nailing

258 Nullify

259 Unlab—to dismantle a scientific laboratory

260 Niches—vertical recesses in a wall to contain a statue

261 Unshod

262 Nation

263 Unjam

264 Injure

265 Unshell—to extract a living organism from its shell

266 Nosh shop—imagine a corner drug store or something similar

267 No joke—a joke that falls flat

268 Unshaved

269 Unship—imagine a great crowd of people being ordered off a ship

270 Necks

271 Naked

272 Noggin—a small mug and/or its contents

273 Income

274 Anchor

275 Nickel—a gray metal related to cobalt; a coin worth 5 cents

276 No cash—imagine someone fumbling in his pockets in order to pay a restaurant bill

277 Knocking

278 Encave—to confine to a dark place; to keep in a cave

279 Uncap—imagine schoolboys stealing one another's caps

280 Nephews

281 Nevada

282 Uneven

283 Unfirm

284 Never

285 Navel

286 Knavish—having the characteristics of a roguish trickster; a deceitful and dishonest man

287 Invoke—to address in prayer; to implore assistance or protection

288 Unfavorable

289 Enfeeble—to make extremely weak and unable to function

290 Nibs

291 Unpod—to take from the pod, as peas

292 New pan—imagine a brilliantly shiny frying pan

293 New beam—imagine the first beam ever from the sun

294   Neighbor

295   Nibble

296   Nippish

297   Unpack

298   Unpaved

299   Nabob—a wealthy person, especially one returned from India with a fortune

300   Moses

301   Mast

302   Mason—one who cuts, builds, and prepares with stone

303   Museum

304   Miser

305   Missile

306   Massage

307   Mask

308   Massive

309   Mishap

310   Midas—the king who craved gold

311   Midday

312   Maiden

313   Madam

314   Motor

315   Medal

316   Modish—in the current style of the fashion

317   Medic

318 Midwife

319 Mudpie

320 Manse—the home of a Presbyterian minister

321 Mend

322 Minion—favorite child, servant, or animal; slave

323 Minim—a creature of the smallest size or importance; a musical note

324 Manner

325 Manila

326 Manage

327 Maniac

328 Manful—brave, resolute, bold; with man's best qualities

329 Monopoly—a popular board game

330 Maims

331 Mammoth

332 Mammon—the Syrian god of riches; worldly wealth

333 My mom

334 Memory

335 Mammal

336 My match

337 Mimic

338 Mummify—to preserve the body by embalming

339 Mump

340 Mars

341 Maraud—to make a plunderous raid; to go about pilfering

342 Marine

343 Miriam

344 Mirror

345 Moral

346 March

347 Mark

348 Morphia—the principal narcotic of opium

349 Marble

350 Males

351 Malt

352 Melon

353 Mile man

354 Miller

355 Molehill

356 Mulish—imagine anything that is characteristic of a mule

357 Milk

358 Mollify—to soften, assuage, appease

359 Mailbag

360 Matches

361 Mashed

362 Machine

363 Mishmash—a jumble, hodgepodge, medley

364 Major

365 Mesh lock—imagine something like a gear cog meshing and locking or a lock that operates by an intricate mesh

366 Magician

367 Magic

368 Much force

369 Much bent

370 Mikes

371 Mocked

372 Mohican

373 Make muck

374 Maker

375 Meekly

376 My cash

377 Making

378 Make off—to hurry away, as a thief from the scene of a crime

379 Magpie

380 Movies

381 Mufti—an expounder of Muhammadan law; civilian dress as opposed to uniform

382 Muffin

383 Movement

384 Mayfair

385 Muffle

386 My fish

387 Maffick—my fake (or fuck!)

388 Mauve feet

389 Movable

390 Mopes—sulks; being dull or out of spirits

391 Moped

392 Embank—to throw up a bank; protect by a bank

393 Wampum—name for money beads and shells used by North American Indians

394 Empire

395 Maple

396 Ambush

397 Impact

398 Impavid—fearless; bold; intrepid

399 Imbibe—to drink in; absorb (often used of liquor)

400 Recess

401 Recite

402 Raisin

403 Résumé—a summing up; a condensed statement; a summary

404 Racer

405 Wrestle

406 Rose show

407 Risk

408 Receive

409 Rasp—to rub with a coarse file; to utter in a grating way

410 Raids

411 Radiate

412 Rattan—Indian climbing palm with a long, thin, many-jointed pliable stem

413 Redeem

414 Radar—imagine "beaming in" on some object in the sky

415 Rattle

416 Radish

417 Reading

418 Ratify—to settle, confirm, approve, establish

419 Rat bait

420 Reigns

421 Rained

422 Reunion

423 Uranium—a radioactive white metalic element

424 Runner

425 Runnel—a rivulet or gutter

426 Ranch

427 Rank

428 Runoff—a decisive final contest; a gutter or spillway

429 Rainbow

430 Remus—one of two brothers suckled by a wolf, one of the mythological founders of Rome

431 Rammed

432 Roman

433 Remember

434 Rammer—an armored point on the prow of a ship

435 Rommel—notorious German war leader

436 Rummage

437 Remake

438 Ramify—to form branches, subdivisions, or offshoots

439 Ramp

440 Roars

441 Reared

442 Rareness

443 Rearman—the last man in a column or file

444 Rarer

445 Rarely

446 Rare show

447 Rearing

448 Rarefy—to lessen the density or solidity of, especially air

449 Rarebit—a dainty morsel; often applied to Welsh rarebit, grilled cheese on toast

450 Release

451 Railed

452 Reloan

453 Realm

454 Roller

455 Reel line—imagine a fishing line tangled on its reel

456 Relish

457 Relic

458 Relief

459 Relapse

460 Riches

461 Reached

462 Region

463 Regime—mode, style, diet; form of government

464 Rasher

465 Rachel

466 Rejudge

467 Raging

468 Arch foe—imagine yourself as a knight with one giant foe among a number of others

469 Reach up

470 Racks

471 Racket

472 Reckon

473 Requiem—a service spoken or sung for the peace of the soul of a dead person

474 Raker—imagine a man who does nothing but rake gardens

475 Recall

476 Roguish

477 Rococo—a highly ornamental, florid style in design

478 Recover

479 Rack up—colloquialism meaning to score points in sport

480 Refuse

481 Raft

482 Raven

483 Reform

484 Reefer—a marijuana cigarette

485 Raffle

486 Ravage

487 Revoke—a card player's failure to follow suit, though he could

488 Revive

489 Roofable

490 Rabies

491 ~~Rabid—furious, violent, unreasoning, mad~~ *Robot*

492 Ribbon

493 Ripe melon

494 Raper

495 Rabble

496 Rubbish

497 Rebuke

498 Rebuff

499 Republic—a society of persons or animals with equality among members

500 Lasses

501 Last

502 Lesson

503 Lyceum—a place for instruction and lectures; a place in Athens where Aristotle taught

504 Laser—a superconcentrated beam of light coming from a vibrating substance

505 Lazily

506 Alsatian

507 Lacing

508 Lucifer

509 Lisp

510 Ladies

511 Lighted

512 Latin

513 Late meal

514 Ladder

515 Ladle

516 Old age

517 Leading

518 Old foe

519 Lead pipe

520 Lance

521 Land

522 Linen

523 Liniment

524 Linear

525 Lineal—relating to a line or lines; in direct line

526 Launch

527 Lank

528 Lunar flight

529 Lineup

530 Looms

531 Limit

532 Layman

533 Lame mare

534 Lamarck—famous French zoologist and botanist

535 Lamella—a thin plate, especially of tissue or bone

536 Lime juice

537 Looming

538 Lymph—a bodily fluid resembling plasma

539 Lamp

540 Layers

541 Lard

542 Learn

543 Alarm

544 Leerer

545 Laurel

546 Large

547 Lark

548 Larva

549 Low Rib—colloquial for "to thrash"

550 Lilies

551 Lilt

552 Lowland

553 Lielow mattress—a camping mattress that serves as a bed

554 Lowlier

555 Lily-livered

556 Lilaceous—like a lily

557 Lilac

558 Low life

559 Lullaby

560 Lashes

561 Legit—colloquial for that which is honest or above board

562 Legion

563 Lush meadow

564 Lecher

565 Lushly

566 All-Jewish

567 Logic

568 Low shot

569 Lush pea

570 Lakes

571 Licked

572 Lagoon

573 Locum—colloquial for a deputy in any office, especially a doctor

574 Lacquer

575 Local

576 Luggage

577 Licking

578 Liquefy—to bring a solid or a gas to a liquid condition

579 Lockup

580 Leaves

581 Livid

582 Elfin—like, or relating to, a fairy or an elf

583 Alluvium—soil deposited or washed down by the action of water

584 Lever

585 Level

586 Lavish

587 Leaving

588 Leave off

589 Lifeboat

590 Lips

591 Leaped

592 Lib now—imagine this phrase as a women's liberation placard

593 Labium—the floor of the mouth of insects and crustaceans, etc.

594 Labor

595 Label

596 Lipchap—a cold sore on the lip

597 Lawbook

598 Leapfrog

599 Lapup

600 Chases

601 Chaste

602 Jason—and the Golden Fleece

603 Chessman

604 Chaser

605 Chisel

606 Cheese show

607 Chasing

608 Joseph

609 Jasper—an opaque variety of quartz, usually red, yellow, or brown

610 Shades

611 Shaded

612 Jetton—an engraved disc or counter

613 Chatham—resort town on Cape Cod

614 Chatter

615 Chattel

616 Chitchat

617 Cheating

618 Shadoof—a water raiser consisting of a long pole hung from a post, and a bucket or bottle, used in ancient Egypt

619 ~~Chat up—to talk to a person of the opposite sex with further contact in mind~~ *Shadowbox*

620 Chains

621 Chant

622 Genuine

623 Chinaman

624 Joiner

625 Channel

626 Change

627 Chink—in the armor

628 Geneva—headquarters for certain United Nations organizations; major city of Switzerland

629 Shinbone

630 Chums

631 Ashamed

632 Showman

633 Jemima—boot with elastic sides, having no laces or clasps to fasten

634 Chimera—a fire-breathing monster with a lion's head, a goat's body, and a dragon's tail

635 Shameless

636 Jimjams—nervous fears; delirium tremens

637 Jamaica

638 Shameful

639 Champ

640 Cheers

641 Chart

642 Shrine

643 Chairman

644 Juror

645 Churl—a surly, ill-bred man

646 Charge

647 Cherokee—North American Indian

648 Giraffe

649 Chirp

650 Jealous

651 Child

652 Chilean

653   Show-loom—imagine an exquisite antique weaving machine put on special display

654   Jailer

655   Shallowly—in a manner not intellectual or lacking in depth

656   Geology

657   Challenge

658   Shelf

659   Julep—with mint

660   Judges

661   Judged

662   Jejune—bare, meagre, empty, attenuated; void of interest

663   Judgment

664   Judger

665   Jewishly

666   Choo-choo-choo—an especially puffy steam engine

667   Joshing—good-natured leg pulling or joking

668   Jehoshaphat—a king of Judah

669   Shoe shop

670   Checks

671   Checked

672   Chicken

673   Checkmate—a position in chess in which the opponent's king is trapped; the end of the game

674   Checker

675   Chuckle

676   Jokish

677   Checking

678   Chekhov—famous Russian author of plays and short stories

679   Jacob

680   Chafes—excites or heats by friction; wears by rubbing

681   Shaft

682   Shaven

683   Chief Mao

684   Shaver

685   Joyful

686   Chiff chaff—one of the British warbling birds

687   Chafing

688   Shove off

689   Shavable

690   Chaps

691   Chapter

692   Japan

693   Chapman

694   Chopper

695   Chapel

696   Sheepish

697 Chipping

698 Sheepfold

699 Shopboy

700 Kisses

701 Cast

702 Casino

703 Chasm

704 Kisser

705 Gazelle

706 Kiss owch

707 Cash

708 Cohesive—with the quality of sticking together, said especially of "sticky tape" and molecules

709 Cusp—the point at which two branches of a curve meet and stop; the pointed end, especially of a leaf

710 Cats

711 Cadet

712 Cotton

713 Gotham—a typical foolish town

714 Catarrh—a discharge from the mucous membrane caused by a cold in the head; the condition resulting from this

715 Cattle

716 Cottage

717 Coating

718 Cadaver—a corpse

719 Cutup—colloquial for *knife fight,* in which one or both antagonists are injured

720 Cans

721 Cant—affected, insincere speech; the fashion of speech of a sect; to speak with whining insincerity

722 Cannon

723 Economy

724 Coiner

725 Kennel

726 Conjure

727 Conk—colloquial for "to bang on the head"

728 Convey

729 Canopy—a covering over a bed or a throne

730 Cameos—pieces of relief carving in stone and agate, etc., with color layers utilized to give background

731 Comet

732 Common

733 Commemorate

734 Camera

735 Camel

736 Gamish—in a plucky or rambunctious mood; of the quality of birds of game

737 Comic

738 Comfy

739 Camp

740 Caress

741 Card

742 Corn

743 Cram

744 Career

745 Carol

746 Crash

747 Crack

748 Carafe—a glass water or wine bottle for the dinner table

749 Carp—to catch at small faults; a freshwater fish usually bred in ponds

750 Class

751 Clod

752 Clan

753 Clam

754 Clear

755 Gaililee—the porch or chapel at the entrance of a British church

756 Clash

757 Clack

758 Cliff

759 Clip

760 Cages

761 Caged

762 Cushion

763 Cashmere—a rich shawl, originally made in Cashmere, India

764 Cashier

765 Cajole—to persuade or soothe by flattery, deceit, etc.

766 Cojudge

767 Catching

768 Cageful

769 Ketchup—tomato sauce

770 Cakes

771 Cooked

772 Cocoon

773 Cucumber

774 Cooker

775 Cackle

776 Quackish—like the call of the duck; characteristic of a charlatan, impostor, or pretender

777 Cooking

778 Quickfire

779 Cockup—colloquial for that which has been made a mess of; improperly arranged

780 Cafés

781 Craved

782 Coffiin

783 Caveman

784 Caviar—a food delicacy; the prepared roe of the sturgeon

785 Cavil—To find objection or needless fault with

786 Gaffish—similar to a barbed fishing spear

787 Caving

788 Cavafy—the "old poet" of Alexandria

789 Coffee bar

790 Cabs

791 Cupid

792 Cabin

793 Cabman

794 Caper—to frolic, skip, or leap lightly, as a lamb; a small berry used for making pickles and condiments

795 Cable

796 Cabbage

797 Coping

798 Keep off

799 Cobweb

800 Faces

801 Fast

802 Pheasant

803 Face mole

804 Visor

805 Facile

806 Visage

807 Facing

808 Phosphor—relating to that which flows or phosphoresces

809 Face up—colloquial for "meet the brunt"; accept the challenge or consequences

810 Fates—the three Greek goddesses of Destiny

811 Faded

812 Fatten

813 Fathom

814 Fetter

815 Fatal

816 Fattish

817 Fading

818 Fateful

819 Football

820 Fans

821 Faint

822 Finance

823 Venom

824 Fawner—an obsequious or sycophantic person; one who insincerely praises for reward

825 Final

826 Finish

827 Fawning—to court favor by cringing

828 Fanfare

829 Vain boy

830 Famous

831 Vomit

832 Famine

833 Fame-mad

834 Femur—the thigh bone

835 Female

836 Famish

837 Foaming

838 Fumeful

839 Vamp—adventuress; woman who exploits men; un-
scrupulous flirt

840 Farce

841 Fort

842 Fern

843 Farm

844 Farrier—a man who shoes horses or treats them for
disease

845 Frail

846 Fresh

847 Frock

848 Verify—establish the truth of, bear out, make good

849 Verb—imagine a word in action itself

850 False

851 Fault

852 Flan—pastry spread with jam or conserves

853 Flame

854 Flare

855 Flail—wooden staff at the end of which a short heavy stick hangs swinging; used for threshing

856 Flash

857 Flake

858 Fluff

859 Flab

860 Fishes

861 Fished

862 Fashion

863 Fishman

864 Fisher

865 Facial

866 Fish shop

867 Fishing

868 Fish food

869 Fish bait

870 Focus

871 Faked

872 Fecund—prolific; fertile

873 Vacuum

874 Fakir—a Muhammadan or Hindu religious devotee

875 Fickle

876 Fake china

877 Faking

878 Havocful—"filled" with devastation and destruction

879 Vagabond

880 Fifes

881 Vivid

882 Vivien—Leigh

883 Fife-man

884 Fever

885 Favillous—consisting of, or pertaining to, ashes

886 Fifish—resembling or having the characteristics of a fife

887 Fifing

888 Vivify—give life to; enliven; animate

889 Viviparous—bringing forth living young rather than in eggs

890 Fibs

891 Fibbed

892 Fabian—employing cautious strategy to wear out an enemy

893 Fob-maker—V.I.P.

894 Fiber

895 Fable

896 Foppish

897 Fee back—imagine yourself receiving money you had paid for a product that was unsatisfactory

898 Fop file

899 Fab boy—colloquialism for a young boy considered very attractive by girls

900 Basis

901 Bast—the inner bark of lime; other flexible fibrous barks

902 Basin

903 Bosom

904 Bazaar

905 Puzzle

906 Beseech—to ask for earnestly; to entreat, supplicate, or implore

907 Basic

908 Passive

909 Baseball

910 Beads

911 Bedded

912 Button

913 Bottom

914 Batter

915 Battle

916 Badge

917 Bedding

918 Beatify—to make happy or blessed; to declare that a person is blessed with eternal happiness

919 Bad boy

920 Bans—curses; interdicts; prohibitions; sentence of out-
lawry

921 Band

922 Banana

923 Benumb—to make numb or torpid, insensible or pow-
erless

924 Banner

925 Banal—trivial, trite, stale, commonplace

926 Bannish

927 Bank

928 Banff—a mountainous area in western Canada in the
Rocky Mountains famous for its beauty and excellent
skiing slopes

929 Pin up

930 Beams

931 Pomade—a scented ointment, originating from apples,
for the hair and skin of the head

932 Bemoan—weep or express sorrow for or over; to lament
or bewail

933 Beam maker

934 Bemire—to get stuck in wed mud

935 Pommel—a rounded knob, especially at the end of a
swordhilt; to beat with the fists

936 Bombshell

937 Beaming

938 Bumph—odds and ends; disorganized stuff; waste, rubbish

939   Bump

940   Brass

941   Bread

942   Barn

943   Brim

944   Barrier

945   Barrel

946   Barge

947   Bark

948   Brief

949   Bribe

950   Blaze

951   Bald

952   Balloon

953   Blame

954   Boiler

955   Balliol—one of the famous colleges at Oxford

956   Blush

957   Black

958   Bailiff—a king's representative in a district; agent or lord of a manor; officer under a sheriff

959   Bulb

960   Beaches

961   Budget

962 Passion

963 Pajamas

964 Poacher—one who trespasses to steal game or fish; a vessel for poaching eggs

965 Bushel—an eight-gallon measure for grain and fruit

966 Push-chair

967 Bushwhacker—dwell in the backwoods

968 Bashful

969 Bishop

970 Bacchus—the Greek god of wine

971 Bucket

972 Bacon

973 Becalm—to still; to make quiet; delay through lack of wind, as a yacht

974 Baker

975 Buckle

976 Baggage

977 Backing—support, moral or physical; a web of strong material at the back of some woven fabric

978 Back off

979 Back up

980 Beehives

981 Buffet

982 Buffoon—a ludicrous figure; a droll clown

983 Pavement

984 Beaver

985 Baffle

986 Beefish

987 Bivouac—a temporary encampment without tents

988 Push

989 Puff up

990 Babies

991 Puppet

992 Baboon

993 Pipe major

994 Paper

995 Babble

996 Baby show

997 Popgun

998 Pipeful

999 Pop-up—an automatic toaster; a toy consisting of a lidded box with sprung puppet

From 1,000 to 2,000 in Ten Easy Steps

It is possible, with ten quick leaps of your imagination, to create a memory system of 1,000 from the basic 100 and a memory system of 10,000 from the basic 1,000. You use exactly the same system as explained in chapter 10, which is simply to coat, cover, or color chunks of your system in different substances, etc. For example, to expand the basic 100 words to a 1,000, using this device, you might use the following system:

100–200	In your block of ice
200–300	All covered in thick oil
300–400	In flames
400–500	Colored a brilliant and pulsating purple
500–600	All made of beautiful velvet
600–700	All completely transparent
700–800	All smelling of your favorite fragrance
800–900	All placed in the middle of a busy highway
900–1,000	All floating on a single cloud in a beautiful, sunny, clear sky

As with all previous systems, practice the Major System privately and with friends. You can probably already begin to sense that the memorization of books, the preparation for examinations, and the like, are becoming increasingly easy tasks. The applications of the Major System are almost as limitless as the System itself and later chapters in the book will show you how to apply it to the memorization of cards, long numbers, telephone numbers, dates in history, birthdays and anniversaries, and examinations.

12

Card Memory System

Magicians and memory experts often amaze and amuse audiences with their ability to remember complete packs of cards in the order in which they were presented. They similarly astound their audiences by being able to rattle off, without any difficulty, the six or seven cards not mentioned when an incomplete "pack" is randomly presented. Extraordinary as these feats may seem, they are not all that difficult and are usually quite straightforward—even though many people accuse the performer of having hidden assistants in the audience, marked cards, and a number of other tricks.

The secret of remembering a complete pack of cards is to attach your Key Memory Image for each card to the Major System you have just learned. All that is necessary to create a Key Memory Word Image for each card is to know the first letter of the word for the suit as well as the number of the card in that suit. For example, all words for the *c*lub cards will begin with *c;* all words for the *h*earts with *h;* all words for the *s*pades with *s;* and all the words for the *d*iamonds with *d.* The second consonant for the card-word will be the consonant represented by the letter from the Major Memory System.

Taking as an example the 5 of *s*pades, you know that it must begin with *s* because it is a *s*pade card, and that its last consonant must be *l* because it is the 5, and 5 in the Major System is represented by *l*. Without much difficulty you arrive at the word *sale,* which represents the 5 of spades. If you wish to devise a word for the 3 of diamonds, it must begin with *d* because it is the diamond suit, and its final consonant must be *m* because *m* is represented by the number 3 in the Major System. Filling in with the first vowel, you arrive at the word *dam,* which is your Image Word for the 3 of diamonds.

Following is a list of the cards (aces count as "one") and their Memory Image Words. A few of the variations will be explained after you have had a chance to familiarize yourself with the list.

CLUBS	DIAMONDS
CA—Cat	DA—Date
C2—Can	D2—Dane
C3—Cam	D3—Dam
C4—Car	D4—Deer
C5—Call	D5—Dale
C6—Cage	D6—Dash
C7—Cake	D7—Deck
C8—Café	D8—Dive
C9—Cab	D9—Dab
C10—Case	D10—Daze
CJ—Cadet	DJ—Deadwood
CQ—Cotton	DQ—Deaden
CK—Club	DK—Diamond

HEARTS	SPADES
HA—Hat	SA—Sot
H2—Hen	S2—Son
H3—Ham	S3—Sum
H4—Hair	S4—Sore
H5—Hail	S5—Sale
H6—Hash	S6—Sash
H7—Hag	S7—Sack
H8—Hoof	S8—Sage
H9—Hub	S9—Sap
H10—Haze	S10—Seas
HJ—Headed	SJ—Sated
HQ—Heathen	SQ—Satan
HK—Heart	SK—Spade

In this system, the jacks and queens have been counted as the numbers 11 and 12, and 10 as *s,* and the king simply as the name of the suit in which he resides. The Memory Words for the clubs are in many cases the same as those for the Major System words for the seventies, but this need not concern you, since the two lists will never come into conflict.

How does the memory expert dazzle his audience? The answer is quite simple: Whenever a card is called out, he immediately associates that card with the appropriate number of his Major System.

If, for example, the first word called out were the 7 of diamonds, you would associate the word *deck* with the first word on your Major System, which is *tea.* You might imagine the entire deck of the boat being covered with swirling tea leaves, or you might even imagine the Boston Tea Party, making sure that in your association you smelled, saw, tasted, and touched as much as you could. If the next card called were the ace of hearts, you would associate the word for this card—*hat*—with the second word on your Major Memory System: *Noah*. You might imagine Noah standing on the arc, wearing a gigantic rain-hat on which was pouring and splashing in the most gigantic volume The Flood. You would actually imagine yourself as Noah, feeling the chill of the water and hearing the splashing, etc. If the next card called were the queen of spades, you would associate the word for that card—*Satan*—with your third Major System word: *Ma*. You might imagine your mother in a titanic struggle with Satan in the burning fires of hell, using as much motion, rhythm, color, and sensuality as possible. Throughout the memorization of a pack of cards using the Major System as the pegs on which to hang the fifty-two items, you can see that you are clearly using both the logical, analytical, sequential, and numerical left side of your brain, and the imaginative, colorful, rhythmical, and sensual right side of your brain. From these few examples, I hope you can see how easy it can be to memorize an entire pack of cards in whatever order they happen to be presented to you. It is a most impressive feat to be able to perform in front of your friends.

Your facility for remembering cards can be taken a step further. It is possible to have someone randomly read you the names of all the cards in the deck, leaving out any six or seven. Without much hesitation, you can name these cards. There are two ways of doing this. The first is to use a technique similar to that explained in chapter 5. Whenever a card is called out, you associate the Image Word for that card within a larger concept, such as the block of ice previously mentioned. When all the cards have been presented, you simply run down the list of card Memory Words, noting those words that are not connected with the larger Memory Concept. If the 4 of clubs had been called, you might have pictured a car sliding across the huge cube of ice or being trapped within it. You could hardly forget this image, but if the 4 of clubs had not been called, you would immediately remember that you had nothing to remember.

The other system for this kind of feat is to mutate, or change, in some way the card Memory Image Word if that card is called. For example, if the king of clubs was called and your image for this was a caveman-like club, you could imagine the club being broken in half. Or if the card called was the 2 of hearts and your normal image for this was a simple farm hen, you might imagine it with an extraordinarily large tail or with its head cut off.

The systems described in this chapter are basic to the remembering of cards, but it does not take much to see that in the actual playing of card games, a Memory System such as this can be of enormous help. You have probably watched people repeating over and over to themselves the cards that they know have been put down or which are in other players' hands, and you have probably seen them sigh with exasperation at their inability to remember accurately.

With your new Memory System, such tasks will become easy and a joy, and whether you use it for serious card playing or simply for enjoyment, throughout the process you will be exercising your creative memory powers and increasing the usefulness of your brain.

13

Long Number Memory System

The long number memory test on page 14 will probably have been particularly difficult (most people, on IQ tests, cannot remember numbers more than 7 or 8 digits in length). Given a long number such as 95862190377 to memorize, most people will try a variety of responses including: to repeat the buildup continually as the number is presented, eventually getting bogged down in the very repetition itself; to subdivide the number into two- or three-number groups, eventually losing both the order and content of these; to work out mathematical relationships between the numbers as they are presented, inevitably "losing track"; or to "picture" the number as it is presented, the picture becoming more and more blurred as the long number is presented.

If you think back to your own performance on the initial long number memory test, you will probably realize that your own approach was either one or a combination of those approaches just mentioned. Once again, the Major System comes to the rescue, making the task of memorizing long numbers not only easy but enjoyable. Instead of using the

Major System as a peg system for remembering lists of 100 or 1,000, etc., you take advantage of its flexibility: Going back to the basic code, and to the Basic Key Image Words you constructed for the numbers from 1 to 100, you use the Key Image Words in conjunction with the Link System to remember long numbers.

For example, take the number at the beginning of this chapter, 95862190377. It is composed, in sequence, of the following smaller numbers, each followed by its Major System Key Image Word:

95—Ball

86—Fish

21—Net

90—Base

37—Mac

7—Key

In order to remember this almost "impossibly long" number, all you now have to do is to use the Basic Link System, making the words into a simple and imaginative little story. For example, you could imagine a brilliant, rainbow-colored ball bouncing with a loud *boing* off the head of a gigantic and beautifully-colored *fish* that had just fought its way out of a very tangled and dripping wet *net,* which was slowly collapsing to the *base* level of the pier, where it wrapped itself around a man, wearing a fawn-colored and wind-blown *mac,* just as he was bending over to pick up the *key,* which had dropped onto the pier with a loud clang.

At the end of this paragraph close your eyes and reenvision the little story you have just created. Now recalling the Key Image Words, transform them into the numbers you will get:

b—9

l—5

f—8

sh—6

n—2

t—1

b—9

s—0

m—3

c—7

k—7

95862190377

It is not essential to remember long numbers using only groups of two. It is just as easy, and sometimes even more easy, to consider the numbers in subgroups of three. Try this with the number 851429730584. It is composed of:

851—Fault
429—Rainbow
730—Cameos
584—Lever

In order to remember this number, which is even longer than the previous number, it is once again a matter of using your Basic Link System to make up a single little image story using your Basic Key Image Words. Using your right-brain imagination, you can imagine some gigantic universal force that could cause a break or a *fault* in beautiful and shimmering *rainbow*-colored *cameos,* which were so heavy they needed a gigantic *lever* to move them. Once again, at the end of this paragraph, close your eyes and refilm the little image story on your inner screen. Now recall the words, and transforming them, you get:

f—8

l—5

t—1

r—4

n—2

b—9

c—7

m—3

s—0

l—5

v—8

r—4

851429730584!

Another system for remembering long numbers, especially if you have not committed the Major Systems Key Image Words to memory, is to improvise with the basic Major System Memory Code, making up 4-consonant words from the number you have to remember. For example, with a 16-digit number, such as 1582907191447620 you could make up the following 4-digit numbers and Key Word Images: 1582—*telephone*, 9071—*basket*, 9144—*botherer*, 7620—*cushions*.

Here you could imagine a loudly and melodically ringing red *telephone* being chucked in a long and graceful parabolic curve into a *basket,* where an annoying person (a *botherer*) is jammed bottom-down (as in comedy films), while other people are throwing multicolored and multimaterialed *cushions* at him. Again, at the end of this paragraph close your eyes and imagine the story, then fill in the words and the numbers in the space below:

If you ever run into difficulty with the order of the words, you can resolve this simply by using, instead of the Link System, either the Number-Shape or the Number-Rhyme System. For example, using the original number at the beginning of this chapter, 95862190377, you would simply link, for example, *ball* to your Key Image for the number 1; *fish* to your Key Image for the number 2; *net* to your Key Image for the number 3; and so on.

You could also use both the Roman Room System and the Alphabet System, simply placing the words you had decoded from the long number either alphabetically or in your Roman Room. Decide which approach to the memorization of long numbers is best for you. Then, to check on the amazing difference this method of number memorization can make, go back to the original Test Chapter, and see just how easy those initial numbers were.

Once you have mastered this skill, you will have not only improved your memory and your creative imagination even further, but will have actually raised your IQ. One subsection of Intelligence Quotient measurements involves the ability to remember numbers. Between 6 and 7 is the average person's limit; a score of 9 or more puts you, in that subsection of the test, in the IQ range of 150 and more!

14

Telephone Number Memory System

Rather than being lodged in memory, most telephone numbers find themselves on scraps of paper in a limitless range of sizes, colors, and shapes, in pockets, drawers, briefcases, and that general storehouse of frustration I call "The Forgettory."

Remembering turns out to be easier than forgetting, and once again it is the Major System that comes to the rescue in this situation. The procedure for remembering telephone numbers is to translate each digit of the telephone number you have to remember into a letter from the basic code of the Major System. Using the letters you have transcribed, you make up little words and phrases from the telephone numbers letters that "link you back" to both the number and the person.

For example, start with the ten people whose numbers you tried to remember in the initial test on page 15.

Telephone Numbers

Your health food store	787-5953
Your tennis partner	642-7336
Your local weather bureau	691-0262
Your local newspaper store	242-9111
Your local florist	725-8397
Your local garage	781-3702
Your local theater	868-9521
Your local discotheque	644-1616
Your local community center	457-8910
Your favorite restaurant	354-6350

In order to memorize these telephone numbers, all you have to do is to translate the numbers of the telephone number into the letters of the Major System, and then to make up catchy and imageful words, phrases, or sentences that use the appropriate letters from the Major System and relate in meaning to the telephone number you are trying to remember. The following examples are possible solutions to these ten telephone numbers.

Your local health food store: 787-5953. This translates into the possible letters *g f g - l b l m. Your memory phrase, starting with each number's letter, could be Good Food Guides: heaLthy Body heaLthy Mind.* In your imagination you would visualize healthy owners of the store, and the Greek ideal of *mens sana in corpore sano,* perhaps even visualizing Olympic Games in which all the participants had bought their food from this health food store.

Your tennis partner: 642-7336. This translates into the letters *sh r n - c m m s.* Your visual memory phrase here might be: *SHows heRoic Net-game - Can Make Masterly Shots.* Again you should visualize your tennis partner making the statement come true.

Your local weather bureau: 691-0262. This translates to the letters: *sh p d - s n sh n*. Here, if you can imagine yourself as a sculptor of the sun, making it into various shapes, and therefore yourself as god of meteorology, you can use a very condensed phrase that includes *only* the letters that translate back into the number: *SHaPeD SuNSHiNe!*

Your local newspaper store: 242-9111. This translates to the letters *n r n - p d t d*. Again, you can use the condensing technique, imagining your local newspaper man shouting, *"News! Read News! - uPDaTeD!"*

Your local florist: 725-8397. This translates to the letters *g n l-f m b g*. Imagine yourself just having given a bouquet of beautiful flowers to the one you love and wanting to shout about it to the world: *"Good News Lovers! Flowers Make Beautiful Gifts!"*

Your local garage: 781-3702. This translates into the letters *c f t - m g s n*. Imagine your garage as super efficient, turning around every car within a day and giving it back to its owner in a condition as perfect as when it came off the assembly line: *Cars Fixed Today! Made Good aS New.*

Your local theater: 868-9521. This translates to the letters *f sh f - p l n t*. Imagine that your local theater is putting on a number of plays by the Royal Shakespeare Company, and that as you attend each of the plays you experience the entire gamut of emotion: *Finest SHakespearian Farces Produce Laughter aNd Tears.*

Your local discotheque: 644-1616. This translates to the letters *ch r r - d j d j*. The latter part needs no changing, so all you have to do in this particular number is to find a little phrase for the first three letters, which is conveniently: *CHanges Revolving Records- DJ! DJ!*

Your local community center: 457-8910. This translates to the letters *r l c - f b d s*. Imagine the whole joint jumping: *Really Lively Community - Football! Baseball! Dances! Swimming!*

Your favorite restaurant: 354-6350. This translates to the letters *m l r - ch m l s*. Again, you can use the condensing approach, imagining your restaurant having won first prize for its excellent cuisine: *My Lovely Restaurant - CHampion MeaLS*.

The examples given above are, of course, very particular, and it will now be up to you to apply the system outlined to the telephone numbers that are important for you to remember. In some cases, the combination of numbers may present a greater than usual difficulty, and appropriate phrases or words may be almost impossible to devise. In such cases, the solutions are still fairly simple. In the first case, you may make up inappropriate words out of the numbers you have to deal with, and then use the basic system, making absurd and exaggerated images to link with the person whose telephone number you are trying to remember. For example, if the telephone number of one of your friends whose hobby is baseball is 491-4276, you would take the Major System word for 49, which is "rape," the Major Word for 142, which is "drain," and the major word for 76, which is "cage." Your image for remembering this number would be of your friend preventing a rape by attacking the attacker with his baseball bat, which in the ensuing confusion fell down a drain, the iron grille of which is similar to the bars of a cage.

Now that you have mastered the basics of the Telephone Number Memory System, it is essential that you associate and link it to your own life. Therefore, in the space provided, make a note of the names and telephone numbers of at least ten people or places you need to remember, and before reading the next chapter make sure you have your own ten numbers firmly pictured in your memory. As you form the images, remember the basic Memory Principles, realizing that the more enjoyable, humorous, and imaginative you make the exercise, the better your memory for those important numbers will be.

My Ten Most Important Telephone Numbers

1. _____
2. _____
3. _____
4. _____
5. _____
6. _____
7. _____
8. _____
9. _____
10. _____

15

Memory System for Schedules and Appointments

As with telephone numbers, many people find appointments and schedules hard to remember. They use similar systems for coping with their problem, the most common, of course, being the daily appointment book. Unfortunately, many people don't always keep their appointment books with them. In this chapter I introduce two systems, the first of which is for immediate daily use, the second for remembering schedules and appointments for an entire week.

The first involves your basic Peg Systems. Simply equate the number in your system with the hour of your appointment. Since there are 24 hours in a day, you can either join shorter systems together, with an appropriate total of 24, or use the first 24 peg words in one of the larger systems.

Let us assume that you have the following appointments:

7—Early morning training

10—Dentist

1—Luncheon

6—Board meeting

10—Late film

At the beginning of the day, which in this case will certainly be no earlier than 5:30 A.M., you run through the list and check for words with associations:

The time for your Early Morning Group Athletic Practice, represented by the Major System word "key," is 7:00 A.M. Imagine your entire team physically unlocking the doors to super health.

At 10:00 A.M. (daze) you have an appointment with the dentist. Imagine him putting earphones on your head that play such soothing music that you are literally in a daze, unable to feel any pain. (What may be interesting in this example is the fact that if you imagine this particular situation, you may actually be able to reduce the pain!)

Your next appointment, at 1:00 P.M. (1300 hours) is for lunch. The key word here is "dam." Imagine your luncheon table and luncheon guests, including yourself, sitting down for lunch at the top of an enormous dam, looking at the limpid lake on one side and the roaring waterfall on the other.

At 6:00 P.M. you have a board meeting. The Major System memory word for 18 (1800 hours) is "Dave." The association here is not difficult: imagine the confidential matters of your board meeting being discussed with the actual members who will be meeting, as well as the "David" of your choice.

Finally, you have an appointment at 10:00 P.M. (2200 hours) to see a late film. The Major System memory word is "nan," so you can imagine going to the film with your grand-mother, or if you like Indian food, imagine yourself eating the large puffy Indian bread (nan) throughout the movie.

You can easily "order" these five appointments, either by using the Link System to link the images you have just made or by simply placing each of the five images on your basic Number-Shape or Number-Rhyme System.

The second system for remembering schedules and appointments may be used for an entire week. As with the memory system for dates, take Sunday as day 1 of the week and ascribe a number to each of the other days:

Sunday   —1

Monday   —2

Tuesday   —3

Wednesday—4

Thursday   —5

Friday   —6

Saturday   —7

Having given a number to the day, you treat the hours as they are in the small system discussed above, and as they appear in railway, shipping, and airline schedules. The day is considered to have 24 hours, from 2400 (midnight) through 1:00 A.M. (0100), noon (1200), 1:00 P.M. (1300), and back to midnight (2400).

Thus, for any hour and day of the week a 2- or 3-digit number is formed—day first, hour second. All that is necessary is to transfer the number into the word of a Major System list. Having arrived at the word, you link it with the appropriate appointment. For example, suppose you had an appointment to see a car you wanted to buy at 9:00 A.M. on Tuesday.

Tuesday is represented by the number 3, which in the Major System translates to the letter *m*. The hour, 9, translates to the letters *b, p*. Referring to the basic list, we see that the key word for Tuesday at 9:00 A.M. is *map*. To remember this appointment, you might imagine the car you are going to see as bursting through a giant map, wrapped in a giant map, or driving across a giant map.

As another example, suppose you have an appointment for a guitar lesson at 5:00 P.M. (hour number 17) on a Thursday (day number 5). The number we derive from Thursday at 5:00 P.M. is 517, the word for this being *leading*. To remember this, imagine yourself leading an entire orchestra with your solo guitar. Make sure your imagination is guided by the Memory Principles and that you can hear all the sounds, feel your guitar, see the orchestra and the audience, etc.

You may think this system a bit cumbersome because it requires a fairly thorough knowledge of the larger numbers in the Major System, but this reservation can be overcome by "rotating" the hours of the day to suit those hours in which you have most appointments. If, for example, your day does not usually start until 10:00 A.M., then 10:00 A.M. can be considered number 1 in your appointment memory system. In this manner, the most important and often-used hours in your day will nearly always be represented by only 2-digit numbers, i.e., the numbers from 10 to 100 in the Major System. As with the daily schedule memory technique, you can "order" your week's schedules by attaching the images, in order, to the Major System. For practical purposes, it is usually best to start on the Daily System first, becoming skilled and familiar with it, and then move on to the Weekly Memory System.

16

Memory System for Dates in Our Century

When you have finished this chapter you will be able to give the correct day of the week for any date between the years 1900 and the present!

Two systems may be used, the first of which is faster and simpler and applies to only one given year, whereas the second spans many years and is a little more difficult. These systems owe much to Harry Lorayne, a well-known North American memory expert. Using the first of these systems, assume that you wish to know the day for any given date in the year 1971. In order to accomplish what may sound like a rather considerable feat, all that is necessary is to remember (or jot down) the following number:

377426415375

"Impossible!" you might say, but once this system is explained you will see that it is in fact very clear and easy to operate. The individual digits of the 12-digit number represent the first Sunday for each month of the year 1971. The first Sunday in April, for example, falls on the fourth day of the month, the first Sunday in December falls on the fifth day of the month, and so on. Once you have remembered this number (if you have difficulty, refer back to the chapter on Long Number Memory) you will rapidly be able to calculate the day of the week for any date in the year.

It is best to explain this concept with examples, so let us assume that your birthday fell on April 28, and that you wished to know what day the date represented. Taking the fourth digit from your Memory Number you would see that the first Sunday fell on the 4th. By the process of adding sevens to this initial Sunday date you rapidly calculate that the second Sunday of the month fell on the 11th (4 + 7 = 7); the third Sunday of the month fell on the 25th. Knowing this, you recite the remaining dates and the days of the week until you arrive at the date in question: April 26th = Monday; April 27th = Tuesday; April 28th = Wednesday. In other words, your birthday falls on a Wednesday in the year 1971!

Suppose you wish to know the final day of the year. The process is similar. Knowing that the first Sunday of the last month falls on the 5th day, you add the three sevens representing the following Sundays to arrive at Sunday 26th. Reciting the next few dates and days we get: 27th Monday; 28th Tuesday; 29th Wednesday; 30th Thursday; 31st (the last day of the year)—a Friday.

As you can see, this system can be applied to any year for which you may especially need to know days for dates. All you have to do is to make up a Memory Number for the first Sunday or, for that matter, the first Monday, Tuesday, etc., of each month of the year; add sevens where appropriate to bring you near to the day in question; and recite to that day.

An interesting tip in making use of the Memory Number of one year with relation to surrounding years is that with each year the first date for the days at the beginning of the month goes down one, with the exception of leap years, when the extra day produces a jump of two for the following year. In the years 1969, 1970, 1971, for instance, the first Sunday for January in each of those years fell respectively on the 5th, 4th, and 3rd days of the month.

The second of the two systems to be introduced in this chapter is for calculating the day for any date from 1900 to the present. It is necessary in this system to ascribe to each month a number that will always remain the same. The numbers for the months are as follows:

January —1

February —4

March —4

April —0

May —2

June —5

July —0

August —3

September—6

October —1

November—4

December—6

Some people suggest that these be remembered using associations such as January is the first month, the fourth letter in February is *r*, which represents 4, and so on, but I think that it is better to use the number:

144025036146

making the words *DRaweR, SNaiL, SMaSH* and *TiReD*. These can then be linked by imagining a drawer on which a snail with a very hard shell is eventually smashed after an effort that made you tired. In this way the key numbers for the months can be remembered.

In addition to the key numbers for the months, the years themselves have key numbers, and I have listed them, from 1900 to 1984.

0	1	2	3	4	5	6
1900	1901	1902	1903	1909	1904	1905
1906	1907	1913	1908	1915	1910	1911
1917	1912	1919	1914	1920	1921	1916
1923	1918	1924	1925	1926	1927	1922
1928	1929	1930	1931	1937	1932	1933
1934	1935	1941	1936	1943	1938	1939
1945	1940	1947	1942	1948	1949	1944
1951	1946	1952	1953	1954	1955	1950
1956	1957	1958	1959	1965	1960	1961
1962	1963	1969	1964	1971	1966	1967
1973	1968	1975	1970	1982	1977	1972
1979	1974	1980	1976		1983	1978
1984			1981			

This system is not so easy to master, but with a little practice it can become almost second nature. The method is as follows: Given the month, numerical date, and the year, you add the number represented by the month key to the number of the date, and add this total to the key number representing the year in question. From the total you subtract all the sevens, and the remaining number represents the day in the week, taking Sunday as day 1.

In order to check this system, we will take a couple of examples. The day we will try to hunt down is the 19th of March 1969. Our key number for March is 4, which we must then add to the date in question, which is 19: 19 + 4 = 23. To this total we must add the key number for the year 1969. Referring to the list we find that this is 2. Adding 2 to our previous total we arrive at 23 + 2 = 25. Subtracting all the sevens from this (3 × 7 = 21) we arrive at 25 − 21 = 4. The day in question is consequently the 4th day of the week, which is a Wednesday. The second date is August 23, 1972. Our key number for August is 3, which we add to 23, giving 26. The key number for the year 1972 is 6, which added to 26 gives us a total of 32. Subtracting all the sevens (4 × 7 = 28) from 32 we arrive at 4. The 4th day of the week is a Wednesday, which is the day for August 23, 1972.

The only exception to this rule occurs in leap years, and then only in the month of February. Your calculations will be identical, but for this month only, the day of the week will be one day earlier than the day you calculate. As with other systems, the best way to gain confidence with those discussed in this chapter is to practice them. I suggest that you start with the easier of the two, become skilled in it, and then graduate to the more advanced. If you really wish to amaze your friends (and perhaps even yourself), you can also use this system to project far into the future, to hunt down days in any of the years to come. Try it.

17

Memory System for Important Historical Dates

The two systems you have just learned enable you to remember the day for any date in this century. The next system will assist you in the memorization of significant dates in history. In Chapter 2 one of the memory tests included a list of ten such dates. They were

1. 1666   Fire of London
2. 1770   Beethoven's birthday
3. 1215   Signing of Magna Carta
4. 1917   Russian Revolution
5. *c.*1454   First printing press
6. 1815   Battle of Waterloo
7. 1608   Invention of the telescope
8. 1905   Einstein's theory of relativity
9. 1789   French Revolution
10. 1776   American Declaration of Independence

The method for remembering these or any other such dates is simple; it is similar to the method for remembering telephone numbers. All you have to do is to make a word or string of words from the letters that represent the numbers of the date. In most cases, there is no point in including the one representing the thousand, since you know the approximate date in any case. Let us try this system on the dates above:

1. The fire of London in 1666 practically destroyed the city, leaving it a heap of ashes. Our memory phrase for the date 1666 would thus be *aSHes, aSHes, aSHes!* or *CHarred aSHes Generally*.

2. Beethoven is famous for many musical accomplishments, but perhaps his greatest and most controversial achievement was the Ninth Symphony, in which he included a choir. His style of music made full use of the percussion instruments. Knowing this, remembering his birthday in 1770 becomes easy: *Crashing Choral Symphony*.

3. The signing of the Magna Carta in 1215 marked a new age of sense and reason. To remember this date, we can use the phrase *New Document—Liberalization*.

4. The Russian Revolution of 1917 was an uprising of the people against what they considered oppression. They demanded greater equality in the form of communism. Our memory phrase: *People Demand Communism*.

5. Printing presses are often great rotating machines that churn out thousands of pages a minute. We can imagine a small version of this as the first printing press, in approximately 1454, which can be remembered by the word *RoLleR*.

6. The Battle of Waterloo in 1815 was triumphant for Wellington but can be considered fatal for Napoleon. Once again we use a Memory Word rather than a Memory Phrase to remember the date: *FaTaL*.

7. The invention of the telescope by Galileo in 1608 changed the way in which man saw the sky. Our Memory Phrase: *Changed Sky Focus*.

8. In 1905 Einstein's theory of relativity shed new light on the way in which matter and energy exist. His theory solved a number of puzzles that had occupied man but also gave rise to many more. Our key word: *PuZZLe*.

9. In the French Revolution in 1789 the king was ranged against the people. Hence, we can remember the date by *King Fights People*.

10. The American Declaration of Independence in 1776 marked in America a feeling of optimism and confidence in a new way of life. This can be encapsulated in the one word: *CoCKSure*.

18

Remembering Birthdays, Anniversaries, and Days and Months of Historical Dates

This next system will be easy for you because it makes use of systems you have already learned. It is also easier than most other systems suggested for remembering such items because the large Memory System you have learned—the Major System—may be used as a "key" for the months and days (other systems usually require code names that have to be especially devised for the months).

The system works as follows: Months are assigned the appropriate Key Word from the Major System.

January   —tea

February —Noah

March   —Ma

April   —ray

May   —law

June   —jaw

July   —key

August   —foe

September—Pa

October   —daze

November—Dad

December—Dan

To remember a birthday, anniversary, or historical date, all that is necessary is to form a linked image between the month- and day-words and the date you wish to remember. For example, your girlfriend's birthday falls on November 1st. The key word from the Major System for November is "Dad"; and the key word for 1 is "tea." Imagine your girlfriend giving a gigantic cup of tea to your father!

You wish to remember your parents' wedding anniversary, which falls on February 25th. The key word for February is "Noah"; and the key word for 25 is "nail." Imagine Noah, who "married" the pairs of animals, trying to marry your parents by nailing them together!

Historical dates are just as easy to remember. For example, the date when the United Nations came into formal existence was October 24th. The Major System key word for October is "daze"; and the key word for 24 is "Nero." Imagine a horse dehydrated from the blaze caused by Nero's burning city, running into a situation where there is no strife.

There is one small danger in this system, and this is epitomized by those people who don't forget the date—they forget to remember it! This can be overcome by making a habit of checking through, on a regular basis, your memory links for the coming week or two. The memory system outlined in this chapter can be linked effectively with the previous system for remembering historical dates by year. In this way, you will have provided yourself with a *complete* date-remembering system.

19

Memory Systems for Vocabulary and Language

As I mentioned in my book *Speed Reading,* vocabulary is considered to be the most important single factor not only in the development of efficient reading but also in academic and business success. This is not surprising when one realizes that the size of one's vocabulary is usually an indication of the range of one's knowledge. Since vocabulary is the basic building block of language, it is desirable and necessary to develop methods of learning and remembering words more easily. One of the better ways of accomplishing this aim is to learn the prefixes (letters, syllables, or words recurring before root words), the suffixes (letters, syllables, or words recurring at the end of root words), and the roots (words from which other words are derived) that occur most frequently in the language you are attempting to learn. A comprehensive list of these appears in the vocabulary chapters of *Speed Reading.*

Here are some more tips on how to improve your word memory:

1. Browse through a good dictionary, studying the ways in which the prefixes, suffixes, and roots of the language are used. Whenever possible, use association to strengthen your recall.

2. Introduce a fixed number of new words into your vocabulary every day. New words are retained only if the principle of *repetition*, as explained earlier, is practiced. Use your new words in context and as many times as possible after you have initially learned them.

3. Consciously *look* for new words in the language. This directing of your attention, known as mental set, leaves the "hooks" of your memory more open to catch new linguistic fish!

These are general learning aids to assist your memory in acquiring knowledge of a language. They may be applied to English, as a means for improving your present vocabulary, or to any foreign languages you are beginning to learn. Having established a *general* foundation for learning words, let us be more specific in the remembering of *particular* words. As with other memory systems, the key word is *association*. In the context of language learning, it is well to associate sounds, images, and similarities, using the fact that certain languages are grouped in "families" and have words that are related.

To give you an idea of this linking method, I shall consider a few words from English, French, Latin, and German. In English, you want to remember the word *vertigo*, which means "dizziness" or "giddiness," and in which a person feels as if surrounding objects were turning around. To imprint this word on the memory you associate the sound of it with the phrase *where to go?* which is the kind of question you would ask if you felt that all surrounding objects were rotating about you.

Two words that many people confuse in the English language are *acrophobia*, which is a morbid fear of heights, and *agoraphobia*, a morbid fear of open spaces. The distinction can be firmly established if you associate the *acro* in *acrophobia* with *acrobat* (a person who performs at great height!) and the *agora* from *agoraphobia* with *agriculture*, bringing to mind images of large flat fields (though the Greek word actually means "marketplace").

Foreign languages are more approachable when one realizes that they form groups. Practically all European languages (with the exception of Finnish, Hungarian, and Basque) are part of the Indo-European group, and, consequently they contain a number of words similar in both sound and meaning. For example, the words for father: German, *vater;* Latin *pater;* French *père;* Italian and Spanish, *padre*. A knowledge of Latin is of enormous help in understanding all the Romance languages, in which many of the words are similar. The Latin word for *love* is *amor*. Related to *love* in the English language is the word *amorous,* which means "inclined to love; in love; and of or pertaining to love." The links are obvious. Similarly, you have the Latin word for *god: Deus*. In English, the words *deity* and *deify* mean, respectively, "divine status; a god; the Creator" and "to make a god of."

French was derived from the speech of the Roman legionnaires, who called the head *testa,* a crockery shard, hence *tête,* and the shoulder *spatular,* a small spade, hence *epaule,* etc. About fifty percent of ordinary English speech is derived either directly from Latin (plus Greek) or by way of Norman French, leading to many direct similarities between French and English.

In addition to similarities based on language grouping, foreign words can be remembered in a manner not unlike that explained for remembering English words. Since we are discussing French, the following two examples are appropriate: In French, the word for *book* is *livre*. This can be remembered more readily if you think of the first four letters of the word *library,* which is a place where books are classified and studied. The French word for *pen* is *plume,* which in English refers to a bird's feather, especially a large one used for ornament. This immediately brings to mind the quill pen used widely before the invention of the steel nib, fountain pen, and Biro. The link-chain *plume—feather—quill—pen* will make remembering the French word a simple task.

Apart from the Latin, Greek, and French, the rest of English is largely Anglo-Saxon, going back to German, giving rise to countless words that are practically the same in German and English—*glass, grass, will, hand, arm, bank, halt, wolf,* etc., whereas others are closely related: *light (licht), night (nacht), book (buch), stick (stock),* and *follow (folgen).*

Learning languages, both our own and those of other people, need not be the frustrating and depressing experience it so often is. It is simply a matter of organizing the information you want to learn in such a way as to enable your memory to "hook on" to every available scrap of information.

One way to get a head start in learning a language is to realize that in most languages, fifty percent of all conversation is made up of only one hundred words! If you apply the Major System to a memorization of these basic one hundred words, you are already fifty percent of the way toward being able to understand the basic conversation of any native speaker.

For your convenience, the basic one hundred words in the English language are listed below, and you will find that if you compare them with their counterparts in, say, French, German, Swedish, etc., nearly fifty percent of these are almost the same as in English, with only minor variations in the accent and accentuation of the word.

The 100 Basic Words That Make Up 50 Percent of All Conversation

1. a, an	22. for
2. about	23. from
3. above	24. to go (went; gone)
4. across	25. to get (got; got)
5. after	26. to have (had; had)
6. again	27. he—him—his
7. against	28. her
8. all	29. here
9. and	30. how
10. any	31. I
11. as	32. if
12. at	33. in
13. before	34. into
14. but	35. it—its
15. by	36. to know (knew; known)
16. can	37. like
17. to come (came; come)	38. me
18. to do (did; done)	39. more
19. each	40. most
20. to find (found; found)	41. much
21. first	42. my

43. new
44. no—not
45. now
46. of
47. on
48. one
49. only
50. or
51. other
52. our
53. out
54. over
55. part
56. people
57. place
58. same
59. to see (saw; seen)
60. shall
61. she
62. me
63. so
64. some
65. state
66. still
67. such
68. to take (took; taken)
69. to tell (told; told)
70. than
71. that
72. the
73. their
74. them
75. then
76. there
77. these
78. they
79. thing
80. to think (thought; thought)
81. this
82. through
83. time
84. to
85. under
86. up
87. upon
88. us
89. use
90. very

91. we	96. who
92. what	97. will
93. when	98. with
94. where	99. work
95. which	100. you

Applying the basic Memory Principles to the memorization of these words and others, and using both the left- and the right-side abilities of your brain, you will find that language learning can be the easy and enjoyable task that most children find it to be. Children are not any better at learning languages than adults; they simply open their minds more to the language and are not afraid to make mistakes. They repeat and make associations with the basics, listen more attentively, copy and mime, and generally have a thoroughly good time without as much instruction as we adults think we need.

20

Remembering Names and Faces

Remembering names and faces is one of the most important aspects of our lives, and one of the most difficult. The reason for the difficulty lies in the fact that in most instances the names have no real "connection" to the faces. In earlier ages it was exactly the opposite, and the whole system developed for giving people names was based on memory and association: The man you regularly saw covered in white flour with dough all over his hands was Mr. Baker; the man you regularly saw in his own and everyone else's garden was Mr. Gardener; the man who labored all day over a hot fire pounding metal was Mr. Blacksmith, and so on. As the generations changed and the family name became more and more removed from its original meaning, the task of the memorization of names and faces became increasingly difficult, reaching the current situation in which the name is a word with no immediate associations to the face.

There are two major methods of coping with this situation, each method supporting the other. The first is the Buzan Social Etiquette Method; the second, the Mnemonic Method.

The Buzan Social Etiquette Method For Remembering Names and Faces

The Buzan Social Etiquette Method for remembering names and faces guarantees that you will never again find yourself in a situation where you are introduced rapidly to five people and hurriedly repeat "pleased to meet you, pleased to meet you, pleased to meet you, pleased to meet you, pleased to meet you," having been introduced only to the five pairs of shoes at which you looked in embarrassment because you knew you were immediately going to forget all the names anyway (which you did!).

The Social Etiquette Method requires two simple things of you:

(1) an *interest* in the people you meet
(2) politeness

The method is the same as that which you might find described in a book of etiquette, yet even books on etiquette often fail to realize that the original rules were made not simply to enforce rigid disciplines but to allow people to interact on a friendly basis, which was structured formally only in order to enable the people to meet and *remember* one another. Select from the following Social Etiquette Memory Steps those that will most help you.

THE SOCIAL ETIQUETTE MEMORY STEPS
1. **Mental set.** Before you enter a situation in which you will meet people, mentally prepare yourself to succeed and *not* to fail. Many people enter such situations "knowing" that they have a bad memory for names and faces and consequently set about proving it to themselves. If you "know" that your memory is going to improve, you will notice immediate improvement. When preparing yourself for meeting people, try

to make sure that you are as poised and relaxed as possible and, also, that wherever possible, you have given yourself a two-to-five minute break for preparation.

2. **Observe.** When you are meeting people, make sure you look them straight in the eye. Don't shuffle around, with your eyes on the floor or looking into the distance. As you look at someone's face, be aware of the special facial characteristics, for this will help you also in the second mnemonic approach to the memorization of names and faces. I have included below a "guided tour" from the top of the head to the tip of the chin, enumerating the various characteristics and the ways in which they can be classified and typified. The more you become skilled at the art of observation, the more you will realize just how varied one face is from another.

If you can sharpen your observational powers, you will have made a giant step toward the improvement of your memory. Blank looking, instead of real seeing, is one of the major causes for poor memory and, eventually, for poor eyesight in general.

3. **Listen.** Consciously *listen,* paying attention as much as you possibly can to the sound of the name of the person to whom you are being introduced. This is a crucial stage of the introductory process, at which point many people fail because they were concentrating more on the fact that they were going to forget than on the sound of the name of the person to whom they were being introduced.

4. **Request repetition.** Even if you have heard the name fairly well, politely say something in the order of "I'm sorry, would you mind repeating the name." Repetition is a major memory aid; each repetition of any item you wish to learn greatly increases the probability of your remembering it.

5. **Verify the pronunciation.** Once you have been given the name, immediately confirm, by asking the person to whom the name belongs, if you have the correct pronunciation. Even a person with a name like Smith might prefer that it be pro-

nounced "Smythe." Your asking for the pronunciation confirms your interest and once again repeats the name, increasing the probability of your remembering it.

6. **Request the spelling.** If there is any doubt about the spelling of the name, politely or playfully ask for the spelling, again confirming your interest and again allowing another natural repetition of the name.

7. **Your new hobby—derivations.** With a natural enthusiasm, explain that one of your new hobbies is the background and derivation of names, and politely ask the person to whom you have been introduced if he or she knows anything about the history of his or her own family name. It may surprise you to know that on average fifty percent of people not only know at least some· part of the background of their families' nomenclature but most of them are enthusiastic about discussing it. Once again you will have confirmed your interest in the individual, as well as having laid the ground for more repetition.

8. **Exchange cards.** The Japanese have developed card-exchange as a major social function, realizing how useful it is for memory. If you are really interested in remembering people's names, make sure you have a very presentable card to give them, and in most cases they will give you their own or write the details down for you.

9. **Repetition in conversation.** Carrying the principles of interest, politeness, and repetition further, make sure that during conversations with people newly met you repeat their names wherever possible. This repetition helps to implant the name more firmly in your memory, and it is also socially more rewarding, for it involves the other person more intimately in the conversation. It is far more satisfying for them to hear you say, "Yes, as Mary has just said . . . ," than to hear you say, "Yes, as she [as you point] has just said . . . ."

10. **Repeat internally.** During any little pause in the conversation, look analytically and with interest at the various people who are speaking and about whom others are speaking,

repeating internally to yourself the names that by now will be becoming second nature to you.

11. **Check during longer breaks.** If you have gone to get a drink for someone or for yourself, or for any other reason are momentarily alone in a crowd, spend that time scanning everyone you have met, repeating to yourself their names, the spelling of their names, any background material you have gathered about the names, plus any other items of interest that have arisen during the conversation. In this way, you will be surrounding each name with associations, thus building up a mapped network in your own mind that will increase the probability of future recall. You will be positively using the process described in chapter 24, on re-remembering.

12. **Repetition at parting.** As you say farewell, make sure you use the name of the person to whom you are saying it. Thus, by this time you will have used both the primacy and recency time-aspects of memory as outlined in the graphs on pages 224 and 227, having consolidated both your initial and final moments during the "learning period."

13. **Review:**

    a) *Mental.* When you have parted from the new people, quickly flash through your mind all the names and faces of those you have just met.

    b) When possible (for example, at a party), get photographs (either the formal ones or informal ones) of the event.

    c) *Your names and faces memory diary.* If you are interested in becoming a really Master Memorizer of names, keep a special diary in which you quickly sketch and make a Mind Map (see chapter 23) of the faces of those you have met, the names that attach to them, plus any other Key Image Word information.

    d) *Personal card file.* Keep a personal card file, noting on each card the time, place, and date at which you met the person concerned.

14. **The Reversal Principle.** Wherever possible, reverse the processes through which you have just been. For example, in introductory situations, repeat your own name, give the spelling, and if it seems appropriate even give the background. Similarly, make sure you present, where appropriate, your personal card. Throughout conversations, if you are referring to yourself, use your own name. This will help others to remember you, as well as encouraging them to use their names rather than pronouns during the conversations. In addition to being more polite, this approach will make the entire conversation more personal, enjoyable, and friendly.

15. **Pace yourself.** There is a tendency, because of the stress of the initial meeting situation, for everyone to rush through it. The great names-and-faces memorizors and the founders of social etiquette invariably take their time, making sure that they have said at least one personal thing to everyone whom they meet. The queen of England is a good example.

16. **Have fun.** If you make the learning of names and faces a serious and *enjoyable* game, the right side of your brain will feel far more free and open to make the imaginative associations and connections necessary for good memory. The "better memories" that children have for names and faces are *not* because their minds are superior but simply because they naturally apply all the principles outlined in this book.

17. **The Plus-one Principle.** If you would normally remember only between two to five of thirty people you have newly met, as the average person would, give yourself the goal of *one more* than you would normally remember. This establishes in your mind the principle of success and does not place the unnecessary stress of your trying to be perfect first time out. Apply the Plus-one Principle each time you are in a new situation, and your road to success in the memorization of names and faces is guaranteed.

Head and Facial Characteristics

1. *The Head*

You will usually first meet a person face-to-face, so before dealing with the rundown of separate characteristics, we will consider the head as a whole. Look for the general shape of the entire bone structure. You will find that this can be: a) large; b) medium; or c) small. And that within these three categories the following shapes can be found: a) square; b) rectangular; c) round; d) oval; e) triangular, with the base at the chin and the point at the scalp; f) triangular with the base at the scalp and the point at the chin; g) broad; h) narrow; i) big-boned; or j) fine-boned.

Fairly early in your meeting, you may see the head from the side and will be surprised at how many different shapes heads seen from this view can take: a) square; b) rectangular; c) oval; d) broad; e) narrow; f) round; g) flat at the front; h) flat on top; i) flat at the back; j) domed at the back; k) face angled with jutting chin and slanted forehead; or l) face angled with receding chin and prominent forehead.

2. *The Hair*

In earlier days, when hairstyles used to be more consistent and lasting, hair served as a better memory hook than it does now. The advent of dyes, sprays, wigs, and almost infinitely varied styles makes identification by this feature a somewhat tricky business. Some of the more basic characteristics, however, can be listed as follows:

Men: a) thick; b) fine; c) wavy; d) straight; e) parted; f) receding; g) bald; h) cropped; i) medium; j) long; k) frizzy; and l) color (only in notable cases).

Women: a) thick; b) thin; or c) fine. Because of the variability in women's hairstyles it is not advisable to try to remember them from this characteristic.

3. *Forehead*

Foreheads can generally be divided into the following categories: a) high; b) wide; c) narrow between hairline and eyebrows; d) narrow between temple and temple; e) smooth; f) lined horizontally; or g) lined vertically.

4. *Eyebrows:* a) thick; b) thin; c) long; d) short; e) meeting at the middle; f) spaced apart; g) flat; h) arched; i) winged; or j) tapered.

5. *Eyelashes:* a) thick; b) thin; c) long; d) short; e) curled; or f) straight.

6. *Eyes:* a) large; b) small; c) protruding; d) deep-seated; e) close together; f) spaced apart; g) slanted outward; h) slanted inward; i) colored; j) iris—entire circle seen; or k) iris—circle covered partly by upper and/or lower lid. Attention may also be paid in some cases to the lid above and the bag below the eye, both of which can be large or small, smooth or wrinkled, and puffy or firm.

7. *The Nose*
When seen from the front: a) large; b) small; c) narrow; d) medium; or e) wide. When seen from the side: a) straight; b) flat; c) pointed; d) blunt; e) snub or upturned; f) Roman or aquiline; g) Greek, forming straight line with forehead; or h) concave (caved in). The base of the nose can also vary considerably in relation to the nostrils: a) lower; b) level; or c) a little higher. The nostrils themselves can also vary: a) straight; b) curved down; c) flaring; d) wide; e) narrow; or f) hairy.

8. *Cheekbones*
Cheekbones are often linked very closely with the characteristics of the face when seen front-on, but the following three characteristics are often worth noting: a) high; b) prominent; or c) obscured.

9. *Ears*

Ears are a part of the face that few people pay attention to, and yet their individuality can be greater than any other feature. They may be: a) large; b) small; c) gnarled; d) smooth; e) round; f) oblong; g) triangular; h) flat against the head; i) protruding; j) hairy; k) large-lobed; or l) no lobe. This feature is of course more appropriate as a memory hook with men than with women, because the latter often cover their ears with hair.

10. *Lips:* a) long upper lip; b) short upper lip; c) small; d) thick (bee-stung); e) wide; f) thin; g) upturned; h) down-turned; i) Cupid's bow; j) well-shaped; or k) ill-defined.

11. *Chin*

When seen straight on, the chin may be: a) long; b) short; c) pointed; d) square; e) round; f) double (or multiple); g) cleft; or h) dimpled. When seen from the side, it will be: a) jutting; b) straight; or c) receding.

12. *Skin:* a) smooth; b) rough; c) dark; d) fair; e) blemished or marked in some way; f) oily; g) dry; h) blotchy; i) doughy; j) wrinkled; or k) furrowed.

Other characteristics of faces, especially men's, include the various and varied growth of facial hair ranging from short sideburns to the full-blooded and face-concealing beard with moustache. There is no point in listing all the variations. It should suffice to note that these hirsute phenomena do exist, but that they, like hairstyles and colors, can change dramatically overnight.

The Mnemonic Names and Faces Memory Principle

The Mnemonic Principles for remembering names and faces are identical to those outlined in chapter 4, emphasizing: (1) imagination, and (2) association. The steps are as follows:

1. Make sure you have the clear mental image of the person's name.

2. Make sure you can actually "hear again" the sound of the person's name.

3. Very carefully examine the face of the person to whom you are being introduced, noting in detail the characteristics outlined on pages 183 to 185.

4. Look for characteristics within the face that are unusual, extraordinary, or unique.

5. Mentally reconstruct the person's face, using your imagination in the way that a cartoonist does to exaggerate any noteworthy features.

6. Associate, using your imagination, exaggeration, and the general Memory Principles, any of the outstanding features to the name of the person.

The quickest and easiest way for you to learn the application of these principles is to put them immediately to practice. On the following pages I have doubled the number of faces and names you were asked to remember in the original test on pages 12 and 13. I have given suggestions on how you might apply the principles to remembering the names associated with the first five faces. Look carefully at them and at the remaining fifteen, remembering as many as you can, then test yourself on pages 188 to 195.

Memorization of Faces

If you wanted, for example, to remember the names of the faces on pages 188 to 195, you would simply apply the techniques outlined—looking closely at the faces, finding some characteristics that you could imaginatively associate to the name, and then making your mnemonic image.

For example, *Mr. Burn* has very close cropped and dark hair. You might imagine that his face was a countryside and that his hair was the result of a gigantic bush or forest fire that had *burned* all the vegetation.

Ms. Knight has hair that hangs or "falls," and the structure of her face is like the end of a day—thus Ms. "Night," which would be close enough for you to remember the full spelling of her name. Otherwise you might imagine her bending her head down from the top of a castle, with some valiant knight climbing up her tresses to rescue her.

Mr. Mapley is easy to remember in that his face is deeply furrowed and lined, and that his hair is similarly laced with patterns—thus a map, leading to Mapley.

Ms. Hammond, although she looks like the typical "blonde beauty," also has a jowl structure that could remind you of the best leg of pork—ham!

Mr. Suzuki has particularly pronounced eyebrows, which you could imagine as the flamboyant handlebars of a Suzuki motorbike.

One other point about remembering people: If you are *certain* that you will be meeting a person only once and are not concerned with your long-term memory of the name and the face, it is often useful to use an outstanding item of clothing that the person might be wearing. This method, of course, is no good for long-term memory, since a person will probably not be wearing the same clothes next time. The same point applies to hairstyles and beards, etc.

15

Mr. Mogambi

16

Mr. Knorr

17

Ms. Woodrowe

18

Mr. Kokowski

19

Mrs. Volkein

20

Mr. Cliffe

21

Mr. Momatt

22

Miss Ashton

23

Mr. Mapley

24

Mr. Dewhurst

Ms. Jabanardi

Mr. Suzuki

Mr. Welsh

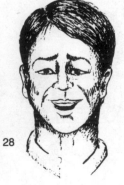

Mr. Macinnes

Ms. Knight

30

Ms. Suzuki

31

Ms. Cook

32

Mr. Pong

33

Mr. Burn

34

Ms. Hammond

30

20

26

23

33

18

29

25

32

24

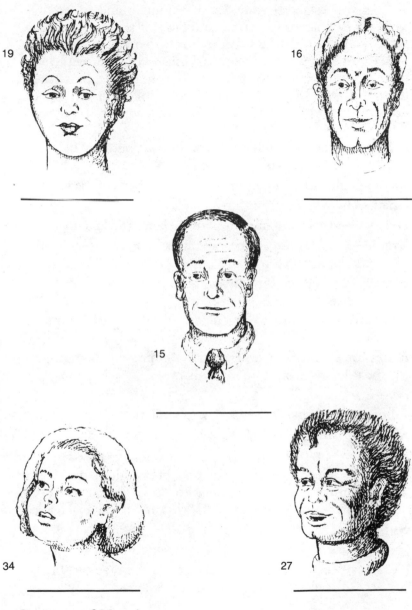

Score out of 20 points: _____

As you establish your Social Etiquette and Mnemonic Memory techniques for names and faces, it is useful to have a Basic Image List of names you are likely to meet. In your Basic Image List simply have a standard image for common names that you can immediately link to the outstanding facial characteristic of anyone who has that name. Following is a list of examples that you can expand to fit your own social context:

Ashcroft—the smoldering roof of a burned-out farm building with masses of flaky gray ash

Blake—a gigantic, limpid blue lake in the shape of the letter *B*

Chalk—the white cliffs of Dover

Delaney—a giant ripping out country lanes (de-lane-ing)

Evans—vans shaped like the capital letter *E*, the spine of the letter being the top of the van

Farren—a tiny little bird *(wren)* seen at a phenomenally far distance

Goddard—God with a particularly "hard" expression on his face

Humphrey—a delighted prisoner humming a happy song as he is let out from behind the bars

Ivy—ivy

Johnstone—a gigantic weight on the toilet!

King—a Memory Principle throne

Lawrence—Arabia!

Mercer—someone pleading for and being given mercy (in certain instances all you need to do is "be close" to the real name and your mind will "click in" to the real name)

Nunn—nun

Ovett—imagine a veterinary surgeon swinging in a gigantic *O*

Patterson—imagine the pitter-*patter* of your own son or the son of someone you know as his little feet scurry across the ground

Quarry—a gigantic and strong-colored open-land mining area

Richardson—picture in your mind the son of a "rich, hard" father

Scott—develop a symbol, such as kilt, haggis; anything typical, for you, of a Scottish person

Taylor—make a suitable image!

Underwood—make sure the wood under which you place the image of the person is memorable, such as an old giant fallen tree, etc.

Villars—a magnificent gleaming white Mediterranean villa

Wade—imagine a person/animal, wading thigh-high through a Lake

Xanthou—a standardized Memory Principle Image of "Thank you"

Young—a springtime image

Zimmermann—an image of someone "zimming" (like skimming/zooming) across the surface of water

Using the Etiquette System, the Mnemonic System, and your standardized name/image system, you will now be well on the way to becoming a master in the memorization of names and faces.

One more magic ingredient can be added to your ability, and it is summarized in an event that changed my life and that largely initiated my own interest in the art and science of memory. The event took place in the first class on the first day of my first year at my university. It was an eight-in-the-morning English lecture, and even the excitement of this first day had not quite managed to shake off the sleepiness in some of our heads. Our professor did. He strode into the room with no briefcase, no writing materials, no notes, and no books, stood in front of the class, announced his name, and then said he would call the roll. Standing in front of the podium with his hands behind his back, he started calling out our names in alphabetical order, going through Adams, Alexander, Barlow, and Bossy, in response to which he got the usual mumbled "yes, sir" and "here, sir." When he came to Camburn, however, there was no reply. He paused for a moment and then said, "Mr. Barry Camburn." There was still no reply. Without change of expression, he then said: "Mr. Barry Camburn, address 29 37 West Eighth Street, phone number 272-73766, born 24th June 1943, father's name Frank, mother's name Mary." The only reply he got was the widening eyeballs and opened mouths of everyone else in the class. Our professor continued calling the roll, and every time he arrived at the name of a person who was absent, he called out the person's Christian name, address, telephone number, birthday, and parents' names.

It was obvious to us that he could in no way have forlearned who was absent, and therefore he must have had *all* of that data on *all of us* totally memorized. When he had completed the roll and everyone was sitting amazed, he repeated very rapidly the names of the students who were absent and said, with a wry smile on his face, "I'll make a note of that sometime."

Though he had never seen any of us, he managed to remember our names and our personal data in perfect order. Using the knowledge you gain from this book, see if you can figure out how he did it. When you have figured it out, apply it, and send me a letter telling me about the result.

21

Memory System for Speeches, Jokes, Dramatic Parts, Poems, Articles, and Books

Speeches

The best way to start approaching the memorization of speeches is to realize that in ninety percent of cases, they do not need to be completely memorized. Realization of this fact will instantaneously help you overcome most of the major problems experienced by those who approach speech writing and speech making as a memory function:

1. The enormous amount of time wasted in preparing a speech for memorization. The average time taken for the preparation and presentation of a one-hour speech is, in total, one week. This wasted time is spent writing, rewriting, and rewriting again and again the speech to make it appropriate

for memorization. The remainder of the wasted time is spent trying to ram, by constant repetition, the speech into the memory.

2. The mental pressure and stress caused by the event.

3. The physical stress resulting from item 2.

4. The relatively stilted presentation that results from a word-for-word memorized presentation.

5. The boredom experienced by the audience who will "sense" that what they are being given is lineally memorized and rigid, and not spontaneous and immediately relevant to them.

6. The aura of stress in both the speaker and the audience, both of whom wait with apprehension for those horrible gaps and pauses that occur when something has been forgotten.

7. The lack of eye contact between the speaker and the audience because the speaker is "looking inward" at the rigidly memorized material and not outward to the audience.

The secret of making a good speech is to remember not the entire speech word-for-word but the main Key Words of your speech. The entire process of preparation and memory/presentation can be made both enjoyable and easy if you follow these simple steps:

1. Generally research the topic about which you are going to speak, making recordings of ideas, quotations, and references that you think will prove relevant. These recordings should be done in the Mind Map form as basically outlined in chapter 23 and as expanded upon in *Use Both Sides of Your Brain* and *The Brain User's Guide*.

2. Having completed your basic research, sit down and plan out, using a Mind Map, the basic structure of your presentation.

3. With your basic structure in front of you, fill in any important details, still in Mind Map form, so that you have

completed a left- and right-brain, associative, imagistic, Mind Map "memory note" of the entire speech. Usually this will contain no more than one hundred words.

4. Practice making your speech from this completed outline. You will find that as you practice, the final order in which you wish to present the speech will become increasingly clear, and you can number the main areas and subtitles of your speech appropriately. You will find that, having completed the research and thought in this way about the structure of the material, you will already have automatically memorized the bulk of your speech. Initially, of course, there will be points in it at which you will hesitate or get lost, but with a little practice you will find that you not only know your speech from beginning to end but know, at a much deeper level than most speakers, the real associations, connections, and deeper structures of your speech. In other words, you will *really* know what you are talking about. This point is especially important, for it means that when you finally do speak to your audience, you will have no fear of forgetting the word order of what you are presenting. You will simply say what you have to say smoothly, using the vocabulary appropriate for the moment and not getting bogged down in a rigid succession of preordained sentence structures. You will thus become a creative and dynamic speaker.

5. As a backup safety system, you can always use one of the basic Peg systems. Select the ten, twenty, or thirty Key Words that completely summarize your speech, use the basic Memory Principles to connect your speech Key Words to the Peg System, thus guaranteeing that even if, for a moment, you do get lost, you will immediately be able to find yourself. Don't worry about any little pauses that might occur in your speech. When an audience senses that a speaker knows what he or she is talking about, a pause is actually more positive than negative, for it makes it obvious to the audience that the speaker is actually thinking and creating on the platform. This adds to the enjoyment of listening, for it makes the presenta-

tion far less formal and more personal and natural. Some great speakers actually use the pause as a technique, maintaining electrifying "thinking silences" of up to as much as a full minute.

In those very rare instances when you do have to memorize an entire speech word-for-word, the process can be made easy by applying everything we have discussed so far in relation to speeches, and then, for the finishing touches, applying the techniques outlined in Dramatic Parts and Poems in this chapter.

Jokes

The problems and embarrassments associated with the memorization and the telling of jokes are almost endless. In recent studies of business people and students, it was found that of the thousands of people questioned, nearly eighty percent thought of themselves as not particularly good joke tellers, all wanted to be good joke tellers, and all listed memory as their major obstacle. The memorization of jokes is actually far easier to deal with than the memorization of speeches because the entire creative aspect of the work has already been done for you. The solution is in two parts: first to establish a basic grid to categorize and capture the main element of the joke; and second, to remember the main details.

The first of these areas is easily dealt with by using a section of the Major System as a permanent library for the stories you wish to file. First, divide the kind of jokes you wish to tell into general categories. For example:

Sex

Animals stories

National stories (Irish, Japanese, etc.)

Rhyming jokes

Toilet jokes

Kids' jokes

"Intellectual" jokes

"Saying" jokes

"Sport" jokes, etc.

List these in numerical preference order and then devote sections of your Major System to these categories. For example, you might have the area from 1 to 10 or 1 to 20 for sexual jokes, the numbers from 10 to 20 or 20 to 40 for national jokes, and so on.

The second area is equally easy to handle; once again it involves your use of the Link System. Let us take, for example, the joke about the man who went into a bar and bought a pint of beer. Having been given his beer, he suddenly realized he had to make an urgent telephone call, but he knew that some of the characters in the bar would swipe his pint before he returned. In order to prevent this, he wrote on the glass, "I am the world's karate champion," and went to make his telephone call, securely thinking that his beer was safe. When he returned, he immediately saw that his glass was empty, and he noticed more scribbling underneath his own. It read: "Thanks for the pint—the world's fastest runner!"

To remember the joke, you consciously select Major Key Words from it, joining them to form the basic narrative. All you need from this entire joke are the Key Memory Words: "pint," "phone," "karate champion," and "running champion."

To complete your memorization, you imaginatively link the first Key Word to the appropriate Key Word in the Major System, and you use the Link System to connect the remaining three Key Memory Words. There are two major advantages to using this system: First, you will be able to clearly remember and categorize whatever jokes you wish; and second, the mass involvement of your right brain in the memorization of the joke itself will make you a far more creative and imaginative joke *teller,* thus overcoming the second major problem for jokers, that of getting in a too rigid and linear, left-brained memorization mode, which bores the listener.

Dramatic Parts and Poems

For the university student, schoolchild, and professional or amateur actor, this aspect of memory can be the most troublesome of all. The method usually recommended and employed is to read a line over and over again, "get it"; read the next line, "get it"; join the two together; "get them"; read the next line and so on and so on ad nauseam until the first lines have been forgotten.

Systems based on the Memory Principles and used successfully by famous actors and actresses are the reverse. In this system the material to be remembered is read and reread quickly (see *Speed Reading*) and with understanding over a period of four days, approximately five to ten times per day. If you read for understanding continually in this way, you will become far more familiar with the material than you realize at the end of the twentieth reading, and you will be able to recall, without looking at the text, most of the material to be remembered. Your mind, especially if you have used your right-brain imagination to help you understand, will have absorbed practically 90 percent of the information, and remembering will have become a natural outgrowth of proper reading and basic understanding using the tools of imagination and association.

This system is far more successful than the line-by-line repetition system, and it can be improved upon even further in the following way: Once again you use Key Memory Words and the Link System. For example, if the material to be remembered is poetry, a few major Key Words will help your mind "fill in" the remaining word-gaps. If the materal to be remembered is part of a script, once again the Key Memory Word Images and Link Systems prove essential. The basic subdivisions of a long speech can be strung together with Key-Word ease, and cues from speaker to speaker can be handled far more effectively if you imaginatively mnemonicize the quantum leap between the previous speaker's last word and your next word. It is lack of the use of these mnemonic techniques that often cause chaos on the stage, especially those long silences and breaks in continuity that occur when one performer forgets his last word or another forgets his first. Acting troupes can save as much as fifty percent of their time, and thus enormously reduce stress and increase enjoyment and efficiency, by applying the Basic Memory Principles to the theatrical works in which they are involved.

Articles

You may need to remember the content of articles on a short-term or long-term basis, and the systems for remembering each are different. If you have to attend a meeting or make a brief résumé of an article you have only recently read, you can remember it almost totally, and at the same time can astound your listeners, by remembering the pages to which you are referring. The method is simple: Take one, two, or three Key Memory Image Words from each page of the article and slot them on to one of your basic Peg Memory Systems. If there is only one Key Word Memory Image per page, you will know that when you are down to Key Memory Image Word number five in your system, you are referring to thc fifth page of the article, whereas if there are two ideas per page and you are at Memory Word seven, you will know you are at the top of page four.

For the memorization of an article over a long period of

time, it will be necessary for you to choose more than two or three Key Memory Image Words per page and to use a more permanent Peg System in conjunction with the review program as outlined in chapter 25.

Books

It is possible to memorize, in detail, an entire book! You simply apply the memory techniques for articles to each page of the book you wish to remember. This is easily done using the Major and Link Systems in combination. Simply take one, two, or three Key Memory Image Words from page one and creatively link them to your Major System Memory Word for Number One: Tea. From page two you select another one, two, or three Key Memory Image Words, creatively linking them to your number two Major System Key Memory Word: Noah, and so on. It will thus be possible for you, in a three-hundred-page book, to remember not only what the basic content of each page was but, if you wish, what each section of each page contained.

22

Remembering For Examinations

You need no longer fear examinations:

- No more the year-long dread that increasingly looms like a storm on the approaching horizon as the year progresses.

- No longer the frantic, rushed, sweaty, frightening final few weeks' and days' buildup of tension before the event.

- No longer the stressful dash into the examination room in order to save every available second.

- No longer the nervous first rush through the examination paper, during which you read so fast that you have to read it again to find out what is actually being asked.

- No longer will you need to spend as much as fiteen to thirty minutes of a one-hour examination jotting down random notes, scratching your head, frowning, frantically trying to recall all that you know and yet at the moment for some reason seem not to remember.

- No longer the frustration of not being able to dig out the essence from the mire of your generally disorganized knowledge.

The common scenario suggested above applies not only to those who know little about the subject but often to those who have a great deal of knowledge. I remember at least three students in my undergraduate years who knew more about certain subjects than practically everyone else in the year and who consequently used to give private tutoring and coaching to those who were struggling. Extraordinarily, these bright students would regularly fail to excel at examination time, invariably complaining that they had not had enough time in the examination room to gather together the mass of knowledge that they had and that for some reason they "forgot" at critical moments.

All these problems can be overcome by preparing for examinations using the techniques for reading and studying outlined in *Use Both Sides of Your Brain* and *Speed Reading*, applying the Mind Map memory techniques as outlined in chapter 23 and especially by using the Major System in conjunction with the Link System. Assume, for example, that the subject you wish to study and prepare to be examined in is psychology. As you study and organize your notes throughout the year, you would consciously and continually build up categories (much as you did when remembering jokes) that contain all the subcategories of the information.

In psychology these categories might include the following:

1. Major headings

2. Major theories

3. Important experiments

4. Significant lectures

5. Important books

6. Important papers

7. General significant points

8. Personal insights, thoughts, and theories

Using the Major System you would allot a certain section to each of these major headings, attaching the Key Memory Image Words from your subjects to the appropriate Major System or Key Memory Word Image. For example, if you had devoted the numbers from thirty to fifty to major psychological experiments, and the fifth of these was an experiment by the behavioral psychologist B. F. Skinner in which pigeons learned to peck for the reward of grain, you would imagine an enormous suit of armor (mail) taking the place of the skin (Skinner) of a giant and warriorlike pigeon who was pecking at the sun, causing to pour from heaven millions of tons of grain.

Using this approach, you will find it possible to contain an entire year's study within the numbers one to a hundred and to transmit this organized and well-understood knowledge into flowing first-class examination papers. If, for example, you were asked, in your psychology exam, to discuss motivation and learning with reference to behavioral psychology, you would pick the Key Words from the question and run them down your Major System Memory Grid, pulling out any items that were in any way relevant to the question. Thus, the general form of your opening paragraph might be as follows:

> In discussing the question of "motivation and learning with reference to behavioral psychology," I wish to consider the following main areas of psychology: blank, blank, and blank; the following five theories: blank, blank, blank, blank, and blank; the following three experiments, which support hypothesis A, blank, blank, and blank; the following two experiments, which support hypothesis B, blank and blank; and the following five exper-

iments, which support hypothesis C, blank, blank, blank, blank, and blank.

In discussing the above, I wish to quote from the following books: blank, blank, and blank; make reference to papers by blank, blank, blank, blank, blank, and blank; include further references from course lectures given on the following subjects: blank, blank, blank, and blank; on the following dates: blank, blank, blank, and blank by Professor X.

And finally, in the conclusion of my answer, I will add a few of my own insights and thoughts in the following areas: blank, blank, blank, blank, and blank.

As you can see, you are already well on the way to a good grade, and at this stage you are still breezing through the introduction to your answer! It is worth emphasizing that in any subject area the last category in your Memory System should be for your own creative and original ideas. It is in this category that the difference between first and second class or scholarship and first class examination results lies.

Besides enabling you to remember information perfectly for examinations, by using the systems outlined in this book, you will also be cultivating the creative powers of your mind that lead to your complete success.

23

Notes for Remembering— Mind Maps

Most people forget what they note because they use only a tiny fraction of their brain, in the note-taking process. Standard note-taking systems use sentences, phrases, lists and line, and numbers. Such systems use only the Basic left-brained Memory Principles of order, sequence and number, leaving out imagination, association, exaggeration, contraction, absurdity, humor, color, rhythm, the senses, sexuality, and sensuality.

In order to make notes well, you have to break with tradition and use both the left and right sides of your brain, as well as all the fundamental Memory Principles. In this system of note taking, you use blank unlined pages, using a Key Memory Image (right brain) that summarizes the central theme of the note you are making. From this central image you have a series of connecting lines (left brain) on which are written (left brain) or drawn (right brain) the Key Image Words or actual images themselves of the main subareas and subthemes you wish to note. Connected to these lines are more lines, again on which you place Key Image Words or

Key Images themselves. In this way you build up a multidimensional, associative, imaginative, and colorful Mind Map Memory Note of everything you wish to note.

Noting in this way, you will not only remember almost immediately and totally everything you write down because of the application of all the Memory Principles to this new multidimensionally mnemonic note-taking approach but you will also find that the approach allows you to understand, analyze, and think critically about whatever it is you are noting, while at the same time it gives you more time to pay attention to either the lecturer or the book from which you are learning. This technique and its applications are more fully outlined in my books *Use Both Sides of Your Brain* and *The Brain User's Guide,* to which I refer you.

As a simple example, an artist summarized the basic outline of *The Brain User's Guide* in a Mind-Mapped Key-Worded and Key-Imaged note that summarized the entire book on a single page (see illustration, page 213). If you combine the Mind-Mapping technique with the remembering for examination approach and use Basic Memory Principles throughout, you are ready to tackle *any* new subject and pass tests with flying colors.

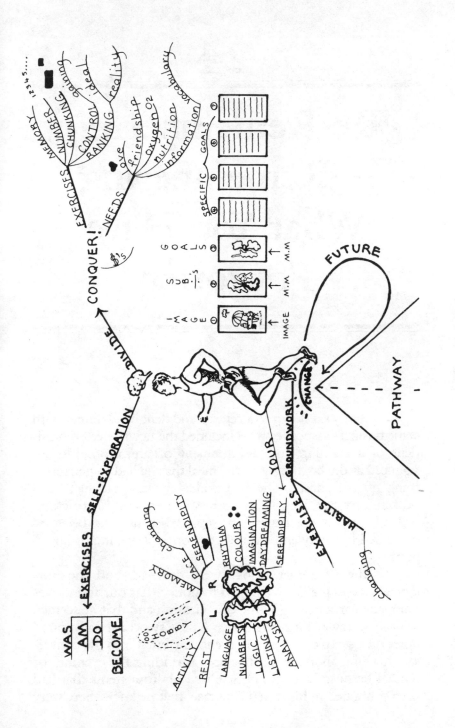

24

Re-Remembering —Remembering What You Have Forgotten

I recently sat down to a relaxed and delightful dinner with some business associates who included the newly elected president of a training and development organization. He announced at the beginning of the meal that he had to get something off his chest or he'd explode: His car had just been broken into, the front windscreen smashed, and his briefcase stolen. He was particularly frustrated because the briefcase contained his diary and a number of other items important to him.

As the predinner drinks were downed, and the hors d'oeuvres completed, we began to notice that our friend was not really participating in the conversation and that he seemed to have a faraway look on his face as he very occasionally jotted notes on a scrap of paper. He eventually burst into the conversation again, announcing that he was ruining the evening for himself because he could remember only four items that had been contained in his stolen briefcase, that he knew there were many more, that he had to give a full report to the police within two hours, and that the more he tried to remember the more blocked he became.

Consider what *you* would have recommended that he do in order to recall.

Several of us at the table who were familiar with Memory Principles then took him through the following exercise: Instead of continuing to allow him to concentrate on what he could not remember (what he in effect was doing was concentrating more and more on the *absence* of memory), we took him through what I call Reliving the Immediate Relevant Past. We asked him when he had last had his briefcase open. It turned out that it was at the office just before he left work, at which point he suddenly remembered that he had put two important magazine articles on the top of the pile in the briefcase. We then asked him when he had last had the briefcase open before leaving home for work. It turned out to have been the previous night after dinner, and he remembered having put two more articles plus a tape recorder and his calculator in, in preparation for the following morning. Finally we asked him to describe the interior design of his briefcase, and as he went through a detailed description of each compartment and section, he remembered pens, pencils, machines, letters, and a number of other items that he had previously completely "forgotten."

Within twenty minutes of what turned out to be a delightful and playful reliving of his previous twenty-four hours in which his frown gradually turned into a broad smile, and in which his physical poise improved, he recalled eighteen additional items to the original four he had recalled after a painful and unpleasant one hour and twenty minutes.

The secret in Re-remembering is to allow the full power of your memory to flow freely without "trying" to remember any one specific thing. The secret within the secret is to "forget about" whatever it is you are trying to remember and to surround the absence (what you have forgotten) with every possible association or connection available to you (see diagram

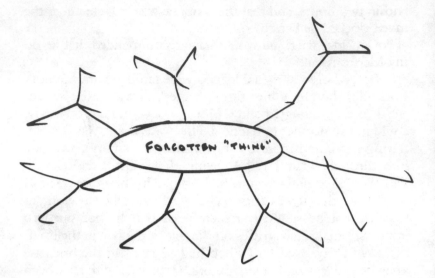

above). Usually the best way to do this is to "relive" all experiences that connect in any way with the item you are trying to remember. This technique works immediately in practically all cases.

In those rare instances where there is not an immediate recall, complete the reliving exercise in exactly the way outlined, and then give your brain the instruction to forget about it on the conscious level but work it out on an unconscious level. You will find that within a few hours or days of this "programming" you will suddenly be taken by surprise—at a meeting, while driving your car, in the shower, on going to sleep or waking, in the bathroom, etc., when your memory supplies the item you have forgotten. This memory technique, like the others, improves all other aspects of your memory as well as your creativity, and in addition gives you a special boost of confidence when you realize that no matter what you have forgotten, you have within the left and right hemispheres of your brain an unconscious Sherlock Holmes who will solve any Memory Mystery you choose to give him!

25

Your Memory's Rhythms

In addition to the Memory Principles you have been applying throughout this book, there are two major areas that, if you understand them, will enable you to double the efficiency of your memory while you are taking in information and then to double it again after you have taken the information in: (1) recall during learning; and (2) recall after learning.

Recall During a Learning Period

In order for you to see clearly how your memory rhythms function during a standard learning period, it will be useful for you to experience a brief "recall during a learning period" yourself. In order to do this, follow these instructions carefully: Read the long list of words below, one word at a time, once only, *without using any memory systems or techniques, and without going back over any words*. The purpose of your reading the list will be to see how many of the words you can remember without using any of the Memory Principles. The order does not matter. So when you are reading the list, simply try to remember as many of the words as you can. Start reading, one at a time, now:

was

away

left

two

his

and

the

far

of

and

that

the

of

beyond

Leonardo da Vinci

which

the

must

and

of

could

the

range

of

and

and

else

the

walk

room

finger

small

change

Now that you have completed reading the list, use the facing page to write down as many as possible of the words you have just completed reading.

Recall During Learning Memory Test

Write down as many as possible of the words you have just completed reading.

Now let's check the way in which your own memory worked: As a general principle, people remember more of what they learn at the beginning and end of a learning period, much more of things that were associated with each other, and always more of those items that stand out in some way.

Thus, the words in this test that are commonly remembered are the first three to five words; the last two or three words; *and, of,* and *the* (remembered because of repetition and linking to themselves), and *Leonardo da Vinci,* because it is outstanding from the rest. In addition, people will remember their own specially associated groups of words within the list, as well as words that for some personal reason are outstanding to them.

It is important to observe what was not remembered: *Anything* that was not at the beginning or end of the learning period, that was not associated to other parts of the learning period, and that was not in any way outstanding. In many cases, this means that the entire bulk of the middle section of the learning period can be forgotten. Relating all of this to yourself and to time, ask yourself the following question: If you had been studying a difficult text for forty minutes, had found your understanding fairly poor throughout, and had noticed that during the last ten minutes of your reading your understanding had begun to improve slightly, would you: stop your studying immediately and conclude that as you had started to do well you could now stop and have a rest; or carry on, assuming that now your understanding was flowing more smoothly, you'd be able to keep it going until it trailed off, and *then* take your break?

Most people choose the latter of these two alternatives, assuming that if their understanding is going well all other things will also be going well. It can be seen from the results of the test you have just taken, and from your own personal experience, however, that understanding and recall are *not* the same. They vary in amounts enormously, and the factor that defines their difference is your own time management.

What you understand you do not necessarily recall, and as time progresses while you learn, you will recall less and less of what you are understanding if you do not in some way solve the problem of the large dip in recall that occurs during the middle of the learning period (see graph, page 224). And this Basic Memory Rhythm applies no matter what you are learning, and that includes the learning of memory systems. What you are looking for is a learning situation in which both recall and understanding can work in maximum harmony. You can create this situation only by organizing the time in which you are learning in such a way as to enable understanding to remain high without giving the memory a chance to sag too deeply in the middle. This is easily accomplished by learning to divide your learning periods into the most beneficial time units. These units, on the average, turn out to be between ten and sixty minutes, as shown in the graph on page 224. If your time is organized in this way, several advantages immediately become apparent:

1. Each of the inevitable dips in your memory during learning will not be so deep as if you had carried on without the break.

2. Instead of only two high points of recall at the beginning and end of the learning period, you will have as many as eight "beginning and ending" high points of recall.

3. Because you are taking breaks, you will be far more rested during your next learning period than you would be had you continued to work without breaks. The additional advantage of this is that when you are rested, both recall *and* understanding function more easily.

4. Because when you are taking breaks you are both more rested and recalling more of each learning session, your comprehension of the next new section in which you find yourself after the break will be greater because you will have laid a firmer foundation in which to nourish and associate the new information. The person who has not taken such breaks,

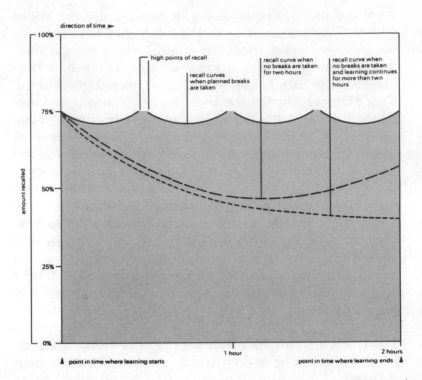

direction of time ▶

high points of recall

recall curves
when planned breaks
are taken

recall curve when
no breaks are taken
for two hours

recall curve when
no breaks are taken
and learning continues
for more than two
hours

100%

75%

50%

25%

0%

amount recalled

▲ point in time where learning starts

1 hour

2 hours

point in time where learning ends ▲

in addition to a growing fatigue, will be recalling less of what
he has learned before, and therefore will be able to make continually fewer and fewer connections between the dwindling
amount of information he has learned and the increasingly
formidable and nonunderstandable information that threatens
him.

5. Contrary to "common sense," your memory of what
you have learned *rises* during the breaks you take rather than
immediately beginning to fall. This rise is due to the fact that

your left and right hemispheres "sort things out" for a little while on an unconscious level after you have finished taking in information during a learning period. When you return to your learning after the break you are therefore actually in possession of *more* conscious knowledge than if you had carried on without the break. This last piece of information is particularly important because it dispels those deep feelings of guilt that you may experience when you find yourself naturally taking a break but at the same time thinking that you ought to be getting "back to the grindstone."

Your breaks should usually be no longer than two to ten minutes. During each break you can allow your mind to rest by going for a short walk, making yourself a light nonalcoholic drink, doing some form of physical exercise, auto-suggesting, meditating, or listening to quiet music.

To consolidate and improve your memory even further, it is advisable at the beginning and end of each learning period to perform a very quick review and preview of what you have learned in the previous learning periods and what you are going to learn in the coming ones. This continuing review/ preview cycle helps to further consolidate the information you already have, gives you growing confidence and success as you progress, allows your mind to direct itself toward the next learning target, and gives you a bird's eye view of the territory you are going to explore mentally during you entire learning session.

Combining your knowledge of the rhythms of your memory in time during a learning period, with the Basic Memory Principles and using your creative imagination, you will be able to form imaginative links and associations throughout your period of study, consequently transforming the sags in the middle of the learning periods into nearly straight lines.

Recall after Learning

Once you have made it easier for your recall to work well during a learning period, it is important for you to do the same thing for your recall after the learning period. The pattern of recall after learning contains two "surprises": First, you retain more of what you have learned *after* a few minutes have passed since the end of your learning period; second, you lose eighty percent of the detail you have learned within twenty-four hours of having learned it. (You can make use of this dramatic fall to help you "take the coats off" your "memory coat hangers" as discussed in chapter 6.) The rise is beneficial, so you want to make use of it; the decline can be disastrous, so you usually need to make sure that it does not happen. The method for both maintaining the rise and preventing the decline is Review by Repetition.

If you have been studying for one unit of time, the high point in your recall after learning will occur approximately one-tenth of a unit afterward. For example, if you have studied for an hour, the high point in recall would be approximately six minutes after you had finished learning. This high point is the ideal time for the first review.

The function of your review is to imprint the information you already have in your mind, in order to make it more "solid." If you manage to review at the first high point, the graph of recall after learning changes, and instead of dropping the detailed information, it is maintained for approximately ten units of time. So, for example, if you had studied for one hour, your first review would take place after six minutes; your second review would take place ten hours later (see graph page 227). From then on, your review should take place only when you feel the information is perhaps slipping away. On the average, these reviews will take place over units of time that are each four times as large as the previous time. So, you would review after one day, then after four days, then after sixteen days, then after forty-eight days, then after ninety-six days, and so on.

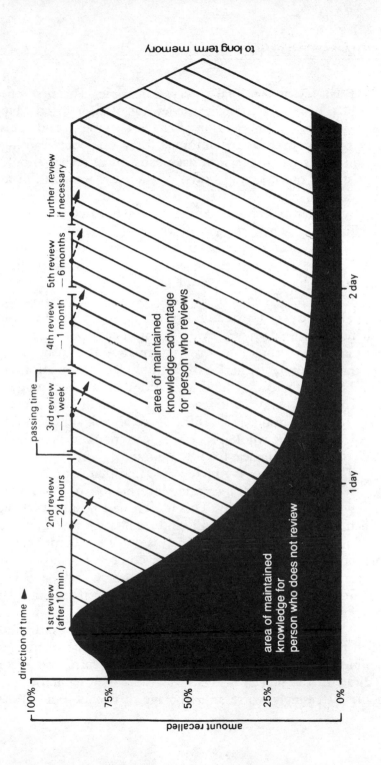

Each review need take very little time. The first one should consist of a complete reviewing of your Mind Map Memory notes or information after the learning period. This may take as much as ten minutes for a one-hour learning period. After the first review, each subsequent review should consist of a quick jotting down of the basic information in your area of interest, and then a comparison of your quick note with your basic notes. Any areas you have left out can be filled in, and any new knowledge you may have acquired during the period between reviews can be added to your original notes. In this manner, your recall of all the information that you need to have constantly available can be guaranteed.

It is useful to compare the mind of the person who consistently reviews with the mind of the person who does not. The person who does not review is continually putting information in and letting that same information drain out. That person will constantly find it difficult to take in new information because the background knowledge he needs to understand that new information will have gone. In such a case, learning will continually be difficult, recall will always be inadequate, and the whole process of learning, understanding, and recall will be unpleasant and arduous.

The person who *does* review will find that with the constantly available store of increasing information, new information will slot in more easily. This will create a positive cycle in which learning, understanding, and recall assist one another, making the continuing process increasingly easy. Surprisingly, the more you learn the easier it is for you to learn more. It is similar to the biblical phrase "to him that hath shall be given, and from him that hath not, even that little which he hath shall be taken away."

This information on recall after learning can also be applied to our current attitudes toward the decline of mental abilities, especially memory, with age. All our current statistics indicate that as human beings grow older their memories become increasingly worse after the age of twenty-four. These findings, substantial as they seem, contain a major fault. They are based on surveys that studied people who generally did not have any information about how their memories worked and who consequently tended to neglect them. In other words, the tests showing that human memory declines with age were performed on people who consistently did not use the Memory Principles and did not review what they had learned. They therefore fell into the second category of the biblical statement.

Recent experiments on people who have applied the Memory Principles and who have properly managed their memory rhythms during and after learning have shown that the *opposite* of the established findings are in fact the case. If you continue to use the numerical, linguistic, analytical, logical, and sequential abilities of the left side of your brain, and if you continue to use the rhythmical, musical, imaginative, colorful, and dimensional abilities of the right side of your brain, along with the Memory Principles and Memory Time Rhythm—all in a continual self-educating approach—your memory will not only *not* decline with age but will actually improve enormously. The more it is fed, the more it will be able to build up imaginative and associative networks with new areas of knowledge, and thus the more it will be able to both remember and create.

The more you give to your memory, then, the more your memory will give back to you, and with compound interest.

26

Catching Your Dreams

Standard ability to remember dreams varies enormously from individual to individual. Some people, in fact, have such bad memories for their dreams that they sincerely believe that they are nondreamers. This is not the case, for research during the past twenty years has shown that every human being has regular periods throughout the night during which dreaming takes place. This is evidenced by Rapid Eye Movement, in which the eyelids flicker and flutter, and occasionally the entire body twitches, as the body internally "sees" and "moves" with the imaginary story. If you have a cat or a dog, you may have noticed this kind of activity while it sleeps, for most higher mammals also dream.

The first step in the memorization of your dreams is the actual retrieval of the dream itself. This you can accomplish by "setting" your mind just before you go to sleep. As you begin to drift off, gently and firmly repeat to yourself, "I will remember my dream," "I will remember my dream," "I will remember my dream." This will "program" your brain to give priority when you awake to the recall of the dream. It may take as many as three weeks before you "catch" your first one, but the process is infallible.

Once you have Caught a Dream, you enter the second stage of Dream Memorization. This is a tricky and "dangerous" moment, for if you become too excited by the fact that you have actually caught one, you will lose it. This is because, for this type of memorization, your brain needs to remain, for a while, in a *nonexcited* state. You must learn to maintain an almost meditational calm, gently reviewing the main elements of the dream. You then very gently select two or three of the Key Main Images from the dream, and attach these, using the basic Memory Principles (which are dreamlike in themselves) through one of your basic Peg Systems.

Let's imagine, for example, that you had dreamed that you were an Eskimo stranded on an iceflow at the North Pole and that you were writing, with gigantic felt-tipped pens, messages for help in the northern sky, forming multicolored words that looked like the aurora borealis. For this you would need only two items from any Peg System. Take, for example, the Alphabet System. In this you would imagine that on the iceflow with you was a gigantic and hairy ape, shivering exaggeratedly in the cold with you and thumping his chest to keep warm as an enormous bee buzzed in and out of the multicolored images you were writing in the sky.

Attaching the Major Dream Images to your Major Key Word System Memory Images in this way allows you to easily span the different brain-wave states in which you find yourself when asleep, when waking, and when fully awake, thus enabling you to remember that important and very useful part of your subconscious life that so many of us hardly ever contact.

Numerous studies completed on people who have started to remember their dreams show that, over a period of months, they become more calm, more motivated, more colorful, more humorous, more imaginative, more creative, and far better able to remember. All of this is not surprising, for our unconscious dream world is a constant playground for the right side of the brain, where all of the Basic Memory Principles are practiced to perfection. Getting in touch with these at the

conscious level encourages all connected skills to improve automatically.

If, as many people do, you become interested in this area of self-exploration and improvement, it is useful to keep a dream diary in Key Memory Word and Key Memory Image Mind Map form (see chapter 23). This diary will give you constant practice in all the skills mentioned and will become an increasingly useful tool in your overall self-development. After a little practice you may well find yourself both appreciating and creating literature and art at levels you had not previously explored. For example, Edgar Allan Poe first remembered and then used the more nightmarish of his dreams as the basis for his great short horror stories. Similarly, Salvador Dali, the great surrealist artist, publicly stated that many of his great paintings were reproductions of perfectly remembered images from his dreams.

It should now be clear to you that the development of memory skills not only gives you the advantage of being able to remember more than you used to but also encourages the total development of the left and right hemispheres of your brain, which leads to a general expansion of memory powers, a burgeoning of your ability to create, and consequently a similar burgeoning of your capacity to appreciate the arts and sciences, to understand yourself and the major areas of knowledge far more easily, and subsequently to contribute creatively to the storehouse of human creativity and knowledge.

Bibliography

Atkinson, Richard C., and Shiffrin, Richard M. "The Control of Short-term Memory." *Scientific American,* August 1971, pp. 82–90.

Baddeley, Alan D. *The Psychology of Memory.* New York: Harper & Row, 1976.

Borges, Jorge Luis. *Fictions* (especially *Funes, the Memorious*). London: Weidenfield & Nicholson, 1962.

Brown, Mark. *Memory Matters.* London: David & Charles, 1977.

Brown, R., and McNeil, D. "The 'Tip-of-the-Tongue' Phenomenon." *Journal of Verbal Learning and Verbal Behavior* 5: 325–37.

Buzan, Tony. *The Brain User's Guide.* New York: E.P. Dutton, 1983.

———. *Make the Most of Your Mind.* New York: Linden Press, 1984.

———. *Use Both Sides of Your Brain.* New York: E.P. Dutton, 1976.

Ebbinghaus, H. *Über das Gedachtnis* (Leipsig: Dunker). Translated by H. Ruyer and C. E. Bussenius. *Memory.* New York: Teachers College Press, 1913.

Haber, Ralph N. "How We Remember What Wc See." *Scientific American,* May 1970, p. 105.

Howe, J. A., and Godfrey, J. *Student Note-Taking As An Aid to Learning.* Exeter, Eng.: Exeter University Teaching Services, 1977.

Howe, M. J. A. "Using Students' Notes to Examine the Role of the Individual Learner in Acquiring Meaningful Subject Matter." *Journal of Educational Research* 64:61–63.

Hunt, E., and Love, T. "How Good Can Memory Be?" In *Coding Processes in Human Memory,* edited by A. W. Melton and E. Martin. Washington, D.C.: Winston/Wiley, 1972. pp. 237–60.

Hunter, I. M. L. "An exceptional memory." *British Journal of Psychology* 68: (1977) 155–64.

Keyes, Daniel. *The Minds of Billy Milligan.* New York: Random House, 1981.

Loftus, E. F. *Eyewitness Testimony.* Cambridge, Mass.: Harvard University Press, 1979.

Luria, A. R. *The Mind of a Mnemonist.* London: Jonathan Cape, 1969.

Penfield, W., and Perot, P. "The Brain's Record of Auditory and Visual Experience: A Final Summary and Discussion." *Brain* 86: 595–702.

Penfield, W., and Roberts, L. *Speech and Brain-Mechanisms.* Princeton, N. J.: Princeton University Press, 1959.

Penry, J. *Looking at Faces and Remembering Them: A Guide to Facial Identification.* London: Elek Books, 1971.

Russell, Peter. *The Brain Book.* London: Routledge & Kegan Paul, 1979.

Standing, Lionel. "Learning 10,000 Pictures." *Quarterly Journal of Experimental Psychology* 25: 207–22.

Stratton, George M. "The Mnemonic Feat of the 'Shass Pollak.'" *Physiological Review* 24:244–47.

Suzuki, S. *Nurtured by love: a new approach to education.* New York: Exposition Press, 1969.

Thomas, E. J. "The Variation of Memory with Time for Information Appearing During a Lecture." *Studies in Adult Education,* April 1972, pp. 57–62.

Tulving, E. "The Effects of Presentation and Recall of Materials in Free-Recall Learning." *Journal of Verbal Learning and Verbal Behaviour* 6:175–84.

von Restorff, H. "Uber die Wikung von Bereichsbildungen im Spurenfeld." *Psychologisch Forschung* 18:299–342.

Wagner, D. "Memories of Morocco: the influence of age, schooling and environment on memory." *Cognitive Psychology* 10 (1978); 1–28.

Yates, F. A. *The Art of Memory.* London: Routledge & Kegan Paul, 1966.